WINGS OF THE GOSPEL

by Rev. John Spillenaar

With Jack Chamberlin

ACTS BOOKS

Published by
ACTS BOOKS
2165 Devlin Dr.
Burlington, On. L7P 3C6

PRINTED IN CANADA
ISBN 0-88941-007-0

DEDICATION

This book is dedicated to my wife Tyyne, who through her loving kindness and prayers has helped make this work a success for Jesus Christ, and to my four children, Rose, Grace, Daniel and David, our gifts from a loving God.

CONTENTS

Chapter 1. . . .A Mighty Miracle. 7
Chapter 2. . . .Earliest Recollections. 11
Chapter 3. . . .Marriage and Family 20
Chapter 4. . . .Into the Unknown North. 35
Chapter 5. . . .My First Glimpse of Eskimo Igloos. 47
Chapter 6. . . .My First Engine Trouble 50
Chapter 7. . . .Betwix and Between. 63
Chapter 8. . . .People and Places 78
Chapter 9. . . .Bible School. 87
Chapter 10. . . .Northland Mission Post 89
Chapter 11. . . .Baie Comeau, Quebec 92
Chapter 12. . . .Labrador and Newfoundland. 98
Chapter 13. . . .Mike Anderson's Healing 107
Chapter 14. . . .Churchill, Manitoba 109
Chapter 15. . . .Weather Plays Havoc. 112
Chapter 16. . . .Pagwa River 115
Chapter 17. . . .A Quitting Mystery. 117
Chapter 18. . . .To The Land of the Eskimo 124
Chapter 19. . . .Mayday, Mayday, Mayday! 137
Chapter 20. . . .Another Building Project 139
Chapter 21. . . .A Larger Plane and Another Miracle 145
Chapter 22. . . .Attawapiskat - The James Bay Project. . . . 148
Chapter 23. . . .My Retirement, A New Challenge 161

INDEX OF PHOTOS

Food For the Body .... Page 40
Planes and Incidents .... Page 41 to 46
Transportation in the North .... Page 75 to 77
Works for the Lord .... Page 85 to 86
People in the North .... Page 101 to 106

FOREWORD

John Spillenaar is a unique man. He is a pioneer, missionary, evangelist, teacher and friend. On several occasions I have travelled with him throughout the Canadian North and the precious times we have had together, ministering among the native people, have developed in me a profound respect for this great man of God.

Northern Canada is one of the neediest mission fields in the world, yet one of the most neglected. Among the few who have responded to the challenge of taking the message of Jesus' love to these hungry souls, the Spillenaar family stand foremost. Hundreds now testify of finding the Lord through their work. Many report miraculous healings and reunited families because of their new trust in Jesus Christ.

Reverend Spillenaar's whole life is centered around his calling to the North. Whether he's flying "QDH" (quit doubting the highest), preaching in an Indian or Eskimo home, or in one of the northland Churches, he is always fishing for souls. God continues to honour this dedication and the native people anxiously await his arrival with more about Jesus for them.

Your heart will be thrilled as you travel through the years and Canada's far north with John Spillenaar. You'll find anxious moments as you face with him, fourteen different times when his aircraft goes down, as well as times when he has been stranded for several days before being rescued.

Read and see the hand of God active daily in the North.

Reverend Bill Prankard
Bill Prankard Evangelistic Association.

CHAPTER 1

A MIGHTY MIRACLE

"For he shall give his angels charge over thee, to keep thee in all thy ways - they shall bear thee up in their hands, lest thou dash thy foot against a stone - Psalm 91: 11-12

"Jesus, help us! Jesus help us!" I could easily hear the cry of Mrs. Rebecca Tait who was in the rear seat of the 180 Cessna missionary plane with her two children, because the engine had suddenly quit, just after take off and we were skimming along - just above the tree tops.

It was July 27, 1962. I had visited quite a number of Indian settlements throughout the Northland during the past number of days and held services along the way. When I reached Sachigo Lake, the plane had to be refuelled from my aviation gas cache there. During the winter months I usually had the tractor train haul in my gasoline either in ten gallon kegs or forty-five gallon drums. A number of men here at Sachigo volunteered to pump gas in the plane tanks from these ten gallon kegs while I was in the village on business. This was the first time I had not supervised refuelling of the plane. But on my return I was told that all was ready. I had been requested to fly over to Ponask Lake to hold a service for a number of our Christian people engaged in commercial fishing. It was a short hop and I was alone in the plane. Shortly after landing at Ponask Lake the people gathered together for a service. We all enjoyed these times of fellowship and worship as we sang, prayed and read the Word of God together in the open air in the shade of the forest trees.

At the close of this service a woman and two children approached me. Then I recognized Mrs. Rebecca Tait, our pastor's wife from Kasabanica, Ontario, approximately 175 miles east. Rebecca told me she came here with her two children to visit her husband's family, Mr. and Mrs. Isaiah Tait, and that it was time for her to return home in Kasabanica. She asked if I would be flying that way and if so, was there room for her and her two children. I told her that I planned to visit Kasabanica and there was room, but I wanted to leave very soon in order to arrive at Kasabanica before dark.

In a very few minutes the Taits and suitcase were packed in the plane. The wind was blowing quite strong creating whitecaps on the waves. I knew this west wind would assist me as a tail wind to Kasabanica once I became airborne and heading east. We had no difficulty in taking off so I climbed into the wind till our altitude was high enough to clear the small hills and trees. I then swung north, away from the narrow Ponask Lake in a shallow wide circle - and headed east. I immediately trimmed the plane into an easy climb.

It was then the engine quit cold after a couple of coughs and sputters. Here we were, the four of us going downwind, just on top of the trees with a dead engine. It was a terrible moment. I hung on to the steering wheel and tried to steady the plane. Rebecca's cry of 'Jesus help us, Jesus help us,' sounded good to me. As the Word of God says in Proverbs 18: 10, "The name of the Lord is a strong tower: the righteous runneth into it, and is safe." I too began to pray - not out loud - but silently, "Lord, you've helped me twice before when I had engine failure, and this is the third time. Please help us now."

As soon as I prayed that prayer, I felt the black Satanic forces of evil close in upon us and I believe it was Satan himself who said, "Yes this is the third time your engine has quit - but it is three times and you are out." (Just like in baseball). The powers of darkness were so tremendous - and in the natural it seemed only too true: that this third time it was "out" for sure. Being too far from Ponask Lake to return and no water to land on - it appeared inevitable that we would have to crash land into the forest.

Just how long that period of darkness and depression lasted, I don't know, but it seemed an eternity as I struggled to maintain level flight - going downwind in the treetop turbulence.

All of a sudden, the Holy Spirit of God brought a scripture

to my mind. It was Psalm 91: 11, 12, "For He shall give His angels charge over thee, to keep thee in all thy ways. They shall bear thee up in their hands, lest thou dash thy foot against a stone."

I said, "Thank you Lord. This is your promise to me - that you will hold this plane up."

What a relief!! Although in the natural everything was the same, I felt somehow the Lord would perform a miracle. And Praise the Lord, He did! We flew for some distance - level flight - with a dead engine until I noticed a small lake, in fact just a pot hole. The Lord helped me to land that plane, although the pot hole was so small we almost hit the other side before the plane stopped.

Oh praise the Lord! What a miracle working God we serve! What a relief to be down safely! We thanked the Lord for His mercy.

Rebecca then said, "How will we ever get out of here?" She knew we could never take off with this load from such a small space.

I replied, "I feel sure the people on Ponask Lake were watching us and they must have heard the engine quit. If I am not mistaken, in about three quarters of an hour they should arrive with their canoes as I believe this little lake is joined to Ponask Lake by a small creek."

Sure enough, in about forty minutes, three canoes burst into view. As soon as the men saw us alive and well, they broke into tears - but they were tears of joy. They were glad to see us. They watched us take off and heard the engine quit, and thought for sure we had crashed. On the way over in the canoes, they watched for smoke to arise as planes usually burn on impact. But praise the Lord, God intervened and performed a miracle and saved us!

While we waited for the canoes to come, I got out on a pontoon to try to find out why the engine had quit. I tried to drain some gas into an empty can which I carried in the plane in case someone got air sick. Instead of draining gasoline, water came out - a lot of water. So I let the water run out, until only gasoline came out. Then I felt sure that most of the water was drained.

Then I remembered - how the men at Sachigo refuelled the plane for me out of the kegs. When I use the gas out of kegs or drums, I always hold the pump a few inches off the bottom of the container. because there is always water in the bottom and the longer drums stay, before being used, the more water condenses. But the men at Sachigo pumped everything into the gas tanks, water and all.

We emptied the plane and placed the contents in three canoes with Rebecca and her two children. I then started the engine. It sounded good. I taxied around to warm it up, then on to the far side of this small lake. With a prayer to God for help, I pushed in the throttle to the limit; the engine roared as we rose and just cleared the tree tops on the far side. I flew over and landed at Ponask Lake. The people there just cried for joy at the miraculous power of God as I told them what had happened.

CHAPTER 2

EARLIEST RECOLLECTIONS
Psalm 63: 1 "O God, thou art my God, early will I seek thee.

I was born October 7th, 1916 in the City of Toronto, Ontario of Dutch parents who immigrated to Canada from Amsterdam, Holland in 1911. My father, Reinhart Spillenaar was born in Holland on March 10th, 1888 and my mother's maiden name was Cornelia Van Loow.

One of my earliest recollections was when I was sitting in church in St. Catharines with my mother. I must have been about five years of age. After the minister preached his sermon he gave an altar call, inviting people to come forward to invite Jesus into their hearts and lives. My mother turned to me and asked if I wanted to go up. Thank God for mothers who take their children to Sunday School and church and who have a concern for their children's spiritual welfare. I was too young to understand the way of salvation but I recall that the two of us walked up and knelt at that altar and prayed.

Another recollection was also before I started to school and while we still lived in St. Catharines on Louth St. My parents had gone downtown shopping on this Saturday morning and a neighbour boy came over. He was about my age and he invited me to go over and play in his yard. His parents were also away. His father had four Beagle hound dogs tied up in the yard. They were very friendly and allowed us to pet and play with them. Later this boy went into his house and brought out two dishes of ice cream. Boy was that ever good! After we finished eating we took the dishes over to the dogs who licked them real good and clean. We then took the dishes and put them back in the kitchen cupboard.

I remember starting school, Gratham #8 on Pelham Road. One day our teacher let us out of classes and I ran outside to go home. I had to cross Pelham Road which was then being sanded and tarred. But a little sand and tar couldn't stop me and away I ran right through that gooey mess and across the field home. You should have seen the look of horror on my mother's face as she looked at me. She asked me what I was doing home at this hour and I said it was dinner time.

"No", she said, "it's only recess time." I had to change clothes and shoes and get back to school somewhat embarrassed.

From St. Catharines we moved to the small community of Irondale, Ontario. My father purchased a farm there and became pastor of the church at the next village of Gooderham. We had a great time on the farm as we had cows, horses, pigs, chickens, ducks, and geese.

During the winter months I went to school early to start the fires and get our one room school warm before class time. Our teacher was a very dedicated young lady. She had all the grades from one to eleven. It was here that I took grades seven and eight in one year.

One incident stands out in my mind when I must have been about ten years old. The railway went right past our property, in fact the tracks were between our house and the road. One day about one o'clock the section foreman and one of his men pulled their hand car off the track at our driveway to let the train go by. This foreman asked me where my father was.

I said, "He is in the house praying and studying for the church service tonight."

This man must have been an athiest because he said so sarcastically, "Son, you better learn to be a preacher when you grow up because they have such an easy life." Although I was quite young I don't remember if I answered him or not but I surely didn't like his attitude. Down in my heart I knew that some day I would be preaching the gospel. This was even before I had accepted Christ as my Saviour.

For months while attending my father's services I felt that I wanted to be saved. Even in my young heart I knew that if Jesus would come or if I died I was not ready to go to Heaven.

Some people think that when one is born and brought up in a Christian home the children automatically are children of God.

But that is not the case. Each one must personally accept Jesus Christ as Saviour. At last at the age of twelve I accepted the invitation to go forward and pray at the altar in the church at Gooderham. It was there I accepted Jesus into my heart and life.

After completing my years in school, I felt the burden of active, full-time service in the Lord's work become greater and greater. Even while ploughing in the fields with a team of horses, I would go into the bush and cry out to God to help me know His will. While working for a farmer four miles out of my home town of Bancroft, Ontario, I attended special services in the church where my father was pastor. I worked hard all day and walked the four miles into town and back after service in the dark. On many of these nights while walking the four miles back I felt the call of God so strongly, that I left the country road and knelt down in the bush and cried to the Lord to reveal His will to me. These were precious times to me.

While I was working for a farmer T.H. Richardson near Lindsay, Ontario, about fifty miles from home, I really received the assurance that God would help me. This Christian farmer made a practice of family devotions three times a day - morning, noon and night. After reading the scriptures he would pray first, then his wife, then it was the hired girl's turn, and lastly it was my turn to pray. On this special occasion, while the others were praying, the cry of my heart was "Lord give me the assurance that I am in your will. I want to be in your will." This was in depression days and I was working for five dollars a month. Just before my turn to pray, the Lord gave me a vision of a huge eye, with the inscription underneath "I will guide thee with Mine eye." Psalm 32: 83. From that day on, I have been very conscious of the Lord's leading and guidance. At the age of 19, I could not resist the call of the Holy Spirit any longer to enter Gospel work. I told my parents, friends, and the farmer for whom I worked that I was leaving. I was offered a bigger wage to stay but it was no temptation. I was asked where I was going but even that I did not know specifically but I definitely felt the call of God to go North.

Father arranged a farewell service at his church in Bancroft. During this service another young man said he would like to go with me. We set the time of departure for the next morning at 9 o'clock. We packed a few extra clothes in a packsack along with a few Bibles and hymn books, a good supply of tracts and a few dollars in our pockets, and off we started walking.

We had a road map to follow and our general direction was northward. We stopped in at most of the farm houses along the road, witnessing to them about the Lord. We had Bible reading and prayer where possible and left them gospel tracts.

Towards evening each day, we inquired about the possibility of a service for that night. Arrangements were often made to hold such services in a home or school or nearby church. Attendance was good as God used us to proclaim the good news of salvation. Men, women and children responded to the invitation to accept Christ as Saviour.

You may wonder how we travelled as we had no car, no horse and buggy, but we did have two good legs, so we walked for almost two months, always continuing northward.

When our tracts were almost gone, we wrote letters home asking for more to be sent to a town ahead. On arrival, we inquired at the post office for mail and sure enough, letters and parcels of tracts would be waiting for us.

Cars often stopped beside us offering us a ride, but our answer was always "no thank you", because we did not want to miss any homes along the way.

Winter arrived, the weather was cold, snow had fallen but still we walked northward. At times, it was somewhat discouraging and we talked together and wondered if we had to walk for the rest of our lives and if not, how would we know when to stop? How would we know where the Lord wanted us?

I remember on one such occasion we left the road and knelt in prayer in the bush asking the Lord about directions. After prayer, I mentioned to my chum that I felt the Lord still wanted us to keep going north until we were asked to open up a Pentecostal church, (as my father was Pentecostal, I just took it for granted that I was Pentecostal too.)

One Saturday evening we stopped at a home and found a clergyman living there. He asked us many questions about ourselves, etc., then invited us to stay with him and preach in his church the following morning. I remember how nervous I was and doubt if I slept at all the whole night, as I thought of speaking the next morning.

Early the next morning, I made my way down the stairs, literally trembling with fear. At the foot of the stairs I noticed this Motto "Perfect love casteth out fear". Praise the Lord, that was just what I needed and I felt much better.

After the morning service, while still on the platform (God helped us and we had a good service) the minister turned to me and said "stay with us today and preach for us again tonight." So we consented. That night the Lord again gave us a precious service. At the close the minister asked: "If you don't have to leave yet, we would like to announce another service for tomorrow night." Again we consented. This happened Tuesday night as well. Since he didn't ask us to stay and open up another church, we felt it was time for us to move on, which we did.

At long last, we arrived in North Bay. It was cold with lots of snow. At the post office there were letters and more tracts for us from home. My father's letters stated that there was a Pentecostal church in North Bay and to be sure and go there, and then when we were ready to leave North Bay to travel south along another route and visit some of his friends along the way back home.

We found the church in North Bay on a Saturday afternoon. The minister knew my father, and invited us to stay and assist him in the services the next day. We were glad to be among Pentecostal people. The Lord blessed during the Sunday services.

The following morning, I told the pastor that we planned on continuing north. He said, "This is the North, and you can't go further because the roads are blocked with snow." The letter from home requested us to turn south and return home. Now what should we do? The two of us made our way down in the basement. The pastor lived on the top floor, the auditorium was on the main floor and the prayer room was in the basement, and that's where we went. After prayer, I asked my partner what he thought we should do.

He said, "Well, it all looks as if we had better turn back

15

and head for home but, what do you think?''

I said, "The only direction I can get from the Lord is to go north.''

"Okay,'' he said, "I'll go with you.'' We told the pastor of our intention - he shook his head - had a word of prayer with us and we left.

We found a bakery downtown where we bought up a supply of cookies and buns, etc., because our map showed us a distance of sixty-two miles through solid bush without a building. With knee deep snow, we knew it would take a few days to walk through, but off we went. Before leaving North Bay, we checked our map and found a place called Kirkland Lake. We wrote home and asked for more tracts to be sent there.

On the outskirts of North Bay, we visited a few homes for reading and prayer. We left the last house and started to walk up the steep hill north of North Bay. We hadn't gone far when I heard a noise behind us - I turned around and saw a car plowing through the snow trying to gain speed to get up the hill. We stepped off the road and let him pass. He got about three-quarters of the way up the hill, became stuck in the snow and backed up to where we were standing. He opened his window and asked us where we were going.

I said, "To Kirkland Lake.''

"Well,'' he said. "I have an appointment in Kirkland Lake for tonight and the people at North Bay told me I could never make it but I am going to try to get through. Do you fellows want a ride?''

Well, we thought, it was no use walking if we could ride, because there were no homes to visit for at least sixty-two miles so we accepted our first ride. But that driver knew what he was doing. He knew he needed help to get through, so with pushing, pulling, and shovelling snow, we at last reached Temagami, at the end of the sixty-two mile stretch. We thanked our driver for the ride telling him this was where we would get off.

He pleaded with us to stay with him and go to Kirkland Lake, saying that we could return to Temagami later to visit the homes there. At last we consented and we arrived in Kirkland Lake late that night. We were surprised to see such a large gold mining town, instead of a few log cabins which we anticipated. Our driver let us out of the car and he went on to keep his appointment.

I saw a huge sign overhead, "Workers Restaurant". We went in and had our first good meal of the day: Were we hungry! Afterwards we thought "What shall we do next?" I noticed a "Provincial Police" sign up the street.

I said to Oliver, "Let's go in there." Meeting the sergeant at the desk I asked, "Do you know any Pentecostal people in Kirkland Lake?"

He said, "Yes there are some, but I don't know them personally. Why don't you go down to the town police station and they may know them."

Well, at least we were encouraged to know that Pentecostal people lived in this town of 20,000.

At the town police station I asked the same question, "Do you know of any Pentecostal people in Kirkland Lake?"

"Yes," he said, "our janitor, if he is not Pentecostal I'm sure his wife is." He called for the janitor to come to the desk. We found out that his wife was Pentecostal and he invited us to go home with him. His wife was indeed glad to see us. She, in turn, gave us the names and addresses of two Pentecostal families. I remember that it was thirty three degrees below zero F when we called at one of the homes, and it was the last day of November, 1936.

The board walk creaked and groaned with every step as we walked in the frosty air. At last we reached the street and the home we were looking for. We knocked on the door and when the lady answered it we introduced ourselves as "two Pentecostal workers". When she heard that she just threw up her arms and started to praise the Lord in a loud voice, leaving us standing out in the cold.

We didn't feel much like praising the Lord. We were tired and cold and it was now about 11 p.m. so we just looked at her and wondered what it was all about. (You know how some Pentecostal folk act?) Well, at last she quieted down and instead of inviting us in, as we expected her to, she turned around, went into the bedroom and called to her husband who was sleeping.

"Daddy, here are two Pentecostal workers, praise the Lord," she was so elated. It was time for him to get up anyway,

17

as he worked the "graveyard" shift at the gold mine, and I can still see him as he got out of bed and rubbed his eyes and made his way into the kitchen.

His wife repeated the second time," Daddy, here are two Pentecostal workers." It then registered in his mind what his wife had said and he was wide awake in an instant and then he too raised his hands and praised the Lord, while we still stood outside in the cold.

After what seemed a long time, they both quieted down and invited us in. How glad they were to see us. With beaming faces they told us their story. It was now late Monday night and the previous Saturday this Pentecostal man had gone to the radio station and put on a broadcast asking if there were other Pentecostal people in Kirkland Lake and if so, to meet at a certain address the next day at 2 p.m. On that Sunday afternoon, this man, his wife and family came to that address. Another man and his wife arrived, the janitor's wife came, another single girl and a young man. The man, responsible for the broadcast, mentioned that he felt that Pentecostal services ought to be started in Kirkland Lake.

He said, "Maybe one of you can preach," but no one was a preacher. Then he said, "Let's sing some hymns. Can one of you lead in the singing?" Again, they all turned that down. So then he said, "Well, if we claim to be Pentecostals, surely we can pray," so they held a prayer meeting, asking God to please send some Pentecostal workers to open a church in Kirkland Lake. The very next day, we arrived, after travelling for over a whole month, and introduced ourselves as Pentecostal workers. No wonder they threw up their hands in praise to the Lord for answering prayer so quickly - even though they left us standing out in the cold.

After telling us their story they asked, "Will you stay and open a Pentecostal church in Kirkland Lake?" Well, that was just the sign given us away back along the highway weeks before, that we should keep going until we were asked to stop and open a Pentecostal church. And that is where we hung our hats.

We stayed with Brother and Sister Earl Cook that night (or I mean the rest of that night). The next day we went to the

18

address where they had held their prayer meeting. This was the place where two Finnish Pentecostal ladies came from Sudbury some time before to open a Pentecostal work among the many Finnish people of Kirkland Lake. Why not join forces?

CHAPTER 3

MARRIAGE AND FAMILY
"And God blessed them . . ." Gen. 1: 28

One of the two Finnish lady evangelists was a beautiful blonde named Tyyne Nykanen and it wasn't long before we realized that we had much in common. It was a year and two months later on January 15, 1938, that we were united in marriage.

Together, over the next ten years, we travelled over Northern Ontario and Quebec holding gospel services and opening up Pentecostal churches in quite a few of the towns. We usually had services each night in some place and many times even two services a night as well as three services in different places on Sunday.

It wasn't too easy going during those first few years, especially the depression years. We often found ourselves unable to mail a letter as we didn't have the two cents for a postage stamp. But then God would provide in some very unusual way. I remember a time when a certain lady asked my wife to make her a dish of scalloped potatoes. She had eaten at our place previously and we had scalloped potatoes at that time. But now we had no potatoes, nor onions and no flour. We did not tell her that our cupboards were bare. We were out visiting at the time and this same lady asked us to visit one of her neighbours. On our arrival we found these people working in their garden digging potatoes and pulling onions out. As we were leaving these people asked us if we could use some potatoes and onions as they had a bountiful crop. You can imagine our thankfulness as they placed a basket of potatoes, onions and other vegetables in our car.

On our return to the first lady's home she mentioned that her husband had brought home one too many bags of flour for the winter and they had no place to store it. She said they had intended to give it to another clergyman but as we were there she felt that perhaps we could use it. So Praise the Lord we had potatoes, onions, flour and other vegetables. We had just prayed for the Lord to supply this need. We then told her of this miracle how God had supplied our needs and my wife was then able to make the scalloped potatoes. This lady mentioned that she had read of missionaries in foreign lands and how God had miraculously supplied their need, but she said, "This is the first time in my life I've ever seen this happen."

While in Kirkland Lake I realized the need of purchasing a home now since I was married and we also needed a car. My wife Tyyne had an old Plymouth which was pretty well a wreck, and we needed a better one so the Lord opened the way for me to get a job at one of the local gold mines.

There were thousands of men out of work at the time, but after definitely praying about it, I applied for a job and within two days, my number was called and I started to work. During the months that I worked to pay off our home and also our new car, my wife and I wondered if the call of God would be stiffled within us and would I insist on continuing to make good money even after our bills were paid? But even while working underground, during slack times I would go into "blind" drifts and there on my knees pour out my heart to God in intercession for lost souls. The Call of God was very much alive within my heart all that time.

December 9th, 1939 was a memorable day for my wife and I. My job at the gold mine was night shift on the eighteen hundred foot level. I had arrived at work at 7 p.m. the night before. My partner and I worked in a stope, drilling with a machine. Then we loaded the holes with powder and blasted at the end of each shift. At about 2:30 a.m., Dec. 9th, my shift boss came rushing in to our stope and said that I was needed at home immediately. I climbed out of the stope, ran along the drift to the level station where the cage was waiting for me. I was hoisted up to surface and I ran from the head frame to the "dry" where I changed clothes and had a quick shower. I ran all the way home and arrived shortly after 3 a.m. Tyyne was already in severe labour pains and at 4 a.m. a blue eyed, eight and a quarter pound baby girl was born. We named her Rose, Esther. What a joy it was to have a baby to look after and to care for. But also, what a responsibility! We thank God for His help and for supplying all our needs.

After working at the Wright Hargreaves Gold Mine for sixteen months, I left and again launched into an active ministry of gospel work across Northern Ontario and into Quebec. We were able to get a young man to take over the church which we had started in Kirkland Lake.

We travelled by car for weeks at a time, visiting in homes and holding services wherever possible. At times our funds were very low and we returned to our home in Kirkland Lake where I would get a job, either in carpenter work or as a painter, or as a salesman, until we had enough money to go out again in pioneer Gospel work.

The last part of July 1941 found us back in Kirkland Lake. On August 3 a doctor and a nurse arrived at our home early in the afternoon and at 4:15 p.m., Grace Lily arrived weighing eight and a half pounds. Now it was my turn to do all the housework, cooking the meals and even washing clothes. I found that a man can do a lot of house work when we set our minds and wills to it.

In the fall of 1942 we moved to Matachewan, another mining town in Northern Ontario. We had visited here before and had held services and a number of people were interested in the Gospel message and a few had accepted Jesus as Saviour.

I was able to get employment at the Venturies Gold Mine. One of my jobs was to work in the refinery where another man, Dan Rimmington and I were responsible to fire up the furnace and melt the precipitate and pour the gold into brick forms. It was quite a job and we would start early in the morning, and in order to complete the job, had to work till 10 or 11 o'clock at night. Some of the gold was mixed in the slag and we used a hand pick to dig it out. Gold pieces were splattered all over the floor and we had to take a broom and shovel and sweep it up and throw it back in the furnace. During this time we held Sunday School and Church services in a rented store building. A fine group of young people and a fair number of adults attended the services.

22

On Feb. 11th, 1943 at about eleven p.m., Tyyne asked me to call the doctor. She was having labour pains. The doctor could not come right then, but a nurse came to our home at about midnight and gave Tyyne a hyypo. Doctor Fitch arrived at 1:30 a.m., Feb. 12 and Daniel John was born at 5:50 a.m., a strong, healthy baby boy of eleven pounds. Now Rose and Grace had a brother to play with.

In July 1943 we were asked to pastor the church at Timmins and South Porcupine, and after much prayer we agreed to do so. Pastor Fred Riddles came into Matachewan to carry on the work there. On Aug. 11th, 1943 Rev. Frank Cunningham, former pastor at Timmins, brought the keys of the Timmins and South Porcupine Church to us. On Aug. 14th we arrived in Timmins to take up residence at the pastor's apartment at 53 Bannerman Ave. The church was located at the corner of Rea and Commercial Sts. On Sundays we held Sunday School and morning services in the Timmins church, then in the afternoon we drove to South Porcupine, 25 Golden Ave. and held Sunday School and an afternoon service - then back to Timmins for an evening service. Through the week we held prayer meetings and also Young People's service in both churches. On Aug. 25, 1944 we held a business meeting with the congregation of the South Porcupine church to purchase this property for $3,000.00 Heretofore we had rented the pool hall.

We set up a building fund to which our church members and others donated. Money was scarce and offerings were low. It was on Nov. 9th, 1944 we borrowed $1,000.00 from the Imperial Bank at South Porcupine and used this as a down payment on the property. I applied for a $2,000.00 loan from the Pentecostal Assemblies of Canada in Toronto. On Nov. 22 the cheque arrived. The next day I took the cheque to the Bank to cash it so that I could pay off loans which we had borrowed from the church members. It was about 10:30 a.m. that 22nd of Nov. when I entered the bank. I noticed quite a line up of customers so I went to the manager's office. He saw the cheque in my hand and asked if I wanted to cash it.

I said, "Yes, but there's such a line up of people out there." He took the cheque and gave it to the teller asking her to get the money ready. In the meantime he came back into the office to talk with me. Just at the time, a masked man entered the bank with a drawn gun and ordered everyone to "Stick 'em up!" One customer who was somewhat deaf was counting his money as he was leaving the bank. I don't think he heard the gun man, as he continued walking. The robber fired a shot and the man fell headlong out on the sidewalk. The undertaker had just driven up to go in the bank. He didn't hear the shot, but he picked up the man and rushed him to the hospital. He died. The robber got a bag full of money including my $2,000.00 and fled in a waiting car. It's a good thing I had not received the cash, so a couple of days later I returned to the bank and received the $2,000.00. It was quite an experience and for months I had the jitters every time I entered a bank.

April 23rd, 1946 I wrote a letter to Rev. Roy Hunter asking him to come to pastor the church at South Porcupine. In the meantime we had asked Alvin Burmaster of Sault Ste. Marie to come and pastor the Timmins church. Both men had accepted. A surprise farewell party was held for us on April 26th and we moved back to our home in Kirkland Lake. Driving from Kirkland Lake we held meetings in the school at Otto Township, in Charlton, Englehart, Haileybury, Matheson, Cochrane, Kapuskasing, Hearst, Larder Lake, Virginia Town.

August 29th, 1947 at 10 a.m. David Victor our second son was born in the Kirkland Lake hospital weighing 10 pounds. Now we had a balanced family of two girls and two boys - all blondes.

We built the church at Charlton in the summer of 1948. And on October 15, 1948 we moved up to Hearst, Ontario to begin building the church and parsonage there.

During this time I had taken our prescribed Bible course in theology and had received my licence to preach and on July 8th, 1944 was ordained with The Pentecostal Assemblies of Canada.

While building the church and parsonage at Hearst, Ontario, during the winter and spring of 1948 and 49, we held services in Kapuskasing sixty-three miles east and also conducted services in Geraldton one hundred and fifty miles to the west plus holding services in many lumber and pulp wood camps.

During this time, I felt the need of going further north, but how? There were no roads, no railways (only as far as Moosonee, which I visited by train and conducted services along the way in bush camps.) I realized the only way was by plane. But I had never been up in a plane in my life, knew nothing about flying, let alone maintenance and repair of an aircraft. But God had created a vision within me to take the Gospel to the Indians and Eskimos of the north.

I wrote many letters to aeronautical schools, inquiring about taking up flying. One of them sent me a list of manoeuvres which I had to make the plane do, in order to get my pilot's licence. I read on down the list, until I came to the item of "spins". "You must make two spins to the right and two to the left, leave your engine idle and make a correct landing." Oh! Oh! I kinda thought I could possibly learn to do all the other things in the list, but to spin the plane - that was something else. I mentioned this to my wife. Immediately she said, "Don't you think the Lord can help you? Others are doing this for business and you want to fly for the Lord?"

That did it. "Okay," I said, "I'll arrange to be a student in one of these schools." I chose Moody Bible Institute in Chicago, U.S.A.

Paul Robinson, the chief instructor in the aeronautical program, accepted me as a special student, as all the other students were taking theology as well. The total cost was at least $1,000. and could go to $1,500. depending on expenses involved which included room and board for a six-month period. "Now, where could I get that much money?" Money was very scarce back in those days, especially that amount. But we started to save. Every dollar we could spare, we put into the bank for this purpose.

Once in a while I had to withdraw a few dollars to pay for gasoline to be able to conduct services in Kapuskasing and Geraldton. My wife would say, "You shouldn't take that money out of the bank, because that's for your aeronautical course."

"But," I replied, "the Lord may come before I have a chance to go to Chicago and we must preach the Gospel now whenever and wherever we can."

I remember on one occasion we were travelling by train south of Hearst on the Algoma Central Railway to a new camp we had heard about and wanted to take the Gospel there too. We found out where the camp was located and the boss' name, so we started out. The train was pretty well filled and shortly after starting out from the Hearst station, a boy appeared out of the baggage compartment with a large wicker basket filled with chocolate bars, tobacco, gum, etc., to sell to the passengers.

After serving a few of the passengers, he came to one big Finnish man who was obviously drunk. Instead of purchasing something, he jumped up, grabbed the basket from the boy and walked swiftly down the aisle, throwing the contents of the basket to the passengers. The poor little boy tried his best to stop him, but could not. In desperation, he was soon crying uncontrollably at the end of the coach. The big Finn turned to the boy handed him the empty basket and said, "Don't cry, I will pay for it all. How much is it?" The boy replied that he didn't know and would have to go to the baggage car and find out. So he ran down the aisle and into the baggage car. After quite a while he returned and approached the Finn who by now had taken his seat. I could not hear what the boy said, but the man pulled a great wad of bills out of his pocket, peeled one off and gave it to the boy, who ran to the baggage compartment and brought back change.

By this time we reached the spot in the bush where we told the conductor we would be getting off. No station here, but a little building was beside the track. After my wife and I got off, lo and behold that big Finn followed us off the train too. The train pulled out and left the three of us standing there.

He said, "Where do you think you are going?"

I said, "We are going to Oscar Vito's camp to hold a service."

"Well," he boomed, "I'm Oscar Vito." What a shock to us, to be alone with this drunken man.

"The camp is a few miles from here back in the bush and you can ride with me on my gas car," he said. Sure enough, he had a little gas car on a narrow guage railway which would take us to his camp. I dreaded the trip, but what else could we do? So we got on the open car, he started the engine and opened the throttle full blast. Away we sailed, up and down the small hills, around sharp corners hanging on for dear life. I thought for sure that the gas car would jump the tracks, but at last we reached the camp. What a relief!

He said, "You can stay in my camp and I will stay with the men. You come for supper at five o'clock, have your service in the dining camp at seven o'clock." Time for service arrived. He had commanded all the men to attend and sure enough, they did! We tried our best to conduct a service, but the boss thought the men weren't singing well enough and he hollered to them time and again to sing better. I was discouraged and thought, "It's not much use to try to carry on," so after both my wife and I had tried to preach, we announced that the service was over.

Immediately the boss jumped up and said, "You are not finished yet."

"Yes," I said, "we are finished."

"No you're not," he said.

I was dumbfounded, so I asked him why he thought we weren't finished.

He replied, "You forgot something."

"What did I forget?" I asked.

"You forgot to take the collection."

"Well," I said, "sometimes we do take up an offering and sometimes we don't and this is one time when we will not take up an offering."

"Oh," he said, "if you don't take up a collection, I will." He called to one of the men to take a hat and then he hollered to all the men to put something in the hat - so around went the hat and back to the boss. Upon receiving the hat he pulled out that big wad of bills, peeled one off and put it in the hat and then handed the hat to me. Knowing he was drunk, I tried to reason with him, but in vain.

At last I said, "You are drunk, and you don't know what you are doing. You don't know how big the bill is that you put in. You must think that is a $2.00 bill, but it is a $20.00 bill (very seldom had I ever seen a $20.00 bill before).

He said, "You mind your own business and you take this collection." What else could I do? We felt downhearted about the service but we did welcome that offering.

In these services we announced that each of the men would be welcome to come to the Hearst Pentecostal church opening on May 24, 1949. The church was packed full with many people standing. After the dedication service, I announced that for the out-of-town guests who planned to stay for the evening service, we would be serving a lunch in the parsonage and we welcomed all. I greeted the people as they came into the parsonage for lunch. One of these was a big Finn. He shook my hand and appeared to be so happy. I asked him if he was a Christian.

"Yes," he joyfully replied.

I asked him how long he had been saved and where.

He said, "Don't you remember that time you and your wife came to Oscar Vito's camp and held a service?"

I said, "I couldn't forget that service when Oscar was so drunk."

"Well, that's the time I asked Jesus to save me and I accepted Him as my Saviour." Praise the Lord!

Time was swiftly approaching when I had to leave for Chicago. War was on in Korea. Our government did not want to give permission to take $1,000.00 out of the country at one time but did allow me to take $400. and the rest would be sent to me monthly. I went to the bank to check on the account that I was saving up and what do you suppose I had? The big sum of $30.00.

The bank manager asked, "What are you going to use for money?"

I replied, "I do not need the $400. until I cross the border at Detroit."

It was the day before Christmas 1949 that I started for Chicago with $30.00 in my pocket - leaving my wife and four children behind to spend Christmas alone. I arranged to speak at a few of our churches enroute. I was especially looking forward to one of our large churches, as the pastor mentioned to be sure to stop in and have a service on a certain night. Even though the offerings were quite small from our smaller churches, I thought all my worries would be over when I got to that big church.

I was quite excited when I entered that city and made my way to the big church. Sure enough it was open, as it was late afternoon. I went inside and looked around. I found a door with the word "Office" on it, and a light was shining underneath the door. I knocked!

The pastor opened the door and said, "Well, John, it's sure nice to see you, but what are you doing down here?"

I said I was on my way to Chicago to take my aeronautical course and I've stopped in a few churches along the way and am I not supposed to be here for a service tonight?

"Oh, John," he said, "I am sorry but I forgot all about it. There is no service here tonight."

Can you imagine how I felt - after planning on a good service here and getting a good offering to help. But that was a lesson the Lord wanted me to learn - we cannot put our trust in man but we must always keep our eyes on the Lord.

The Lord opened the way to have meetings almost every night and by the time I reached Windsor to cross the border to Detroit, I had $425.00. That was $25.00 over the amount I could take over so I sent the $25.00 to my wife in Hearst, Ontario.

I arrived in Chicago and started my course at the Moody Bible Institute. I remember my very first plane ride. Paul Robinson the chief instructor was at the controls in front, I sat behind, holding on for dear life. In my nervousness, I asked Paul if he was sure that there was enough gas in the plane. He assured me there was. He started the engine and we rolled down the runway. After gathering speed, we took off in a climb. I fearfully looked over the side and saw the earth getting further and further away. What a terrible feeling I had and then I thought, "And I am down here in Chicago to learn to fly one of these things."

With the help of the Lord, I did learn to fly. After soloing, one of my instructors asked me if I would like a cross-country flight up into Canada to my home in Hearst. It was a real thrill as we flew north of Chicago along the western shore of Lake Michigan, across the top, over to Sault Ste. Marie and into Canada then straight north to Hearst. What a thrill to be home again for two days. Our flight back was not so nice. We had bad weather which forced us to land at Hawk Junction, then again on a river just north of the Soo, but we finally arrived back in Chicago where I continued my aeronautical training.

Another one of our cross-country flights was to the Piper Aircraft Factory at Lock Haven, Penn. U.S.A. I met Mr. Piper,

Sr. and told him my desire of getting a plane for the missionary work in Northern Canada. I had my eyes on a four-seater Pacer, the kind we had flown with, but Mr. Piper advised against that kind of a plane.

"Your best plane for up there would be the Super Cub," he said. He also mentioned many extras to go on the plane, needed for such a work - quick oil drain for the cold winters, skiis for winter, floats for summer, rust-proofing throughout. With tax and duty and all those extras, he figured the cost would be near the $7,000.00 mark. By this time, I was quite excited about their Super Cub and I asked Mr. Piper quite a few questions, but I noticed that he tried a few times to ask me something. As I now was doing most of the talking, he didn't get much of a chance.

Just before we left he did manage to ask me the question that was bothering him - "How will you pay for this plane." Oh, Oh, why should he bring this up, I thought? Then in a flash the Lord gave me the answer.

"Oh, I said, "we'll pay cash."

"Fine," he said, "then, there will be no problem. Just let us know three or four weeks ahead of time when you will need the plane and we'll put all the extras on it."

Just before my six months course was up, (as I took not only flying but navigation, meteorology, maintenance, repairs, overhaul of engines and craft,) the first plane accident happened at the Elmhurst airport. One of our instructors lived near Paul Robinson's home where I roomed and boarded. He would pick me up one day with his car and we would drive to the airport together. Then the next day, he and I would take my car.

On this particular day, Dick used his car and at closing time that evening, Dick said, "John, you take my car over to the other airfield. I am going to fly over, with three other students and I'll meet you there."

Off I drove, knowing it would take me much longer to drive than a plane could fly. I was at the airport and no Dick or plane was in sight. I waited and waited until the phone rang and I was informed to come back to our airfield as there was a plane accident. I rushed back and arrived in time to see the firemen dragging four burned bodies out of the wreckage. Dick was one. It was a terrible sight. Other students and instructors were among the crowd.

One of the instructors told me later, "John, when I saw you as white as a sheet watching the firemen pull those bodies out of the burnt wreckage I thought to myself that you would never want to fly again."

I arrived home in June, 1950. I could fly a plane but still I could not get my Canadian licence, until I learned how to spin, as spins were not required in the States, but were then required in Canada.

I arranged to take spins at a flying school in Toronto. After checking out my flying, the instructor said, "Oh, you'll have no trouble at all. Just a few lessons and you'll have it. How much time have you got to spend with us?" I said that I could stay till I got my Canadian licence. "Okay," he said, 'I'll have arrangements made to have the Inspector here for your test on Friday." This was Monday so he said to be back for Tuesday to start my spin lessons. I arrived Tuesday morning. He was busy with other students, but in the afternoon, I went up with him. He flew the plane up to 3000 feet with me beside him. He told me to watch him carefully as he flipped the plane over in a right hand spin. Man, what a feeling I had as we spun earthward. At about 1000 feet we recovered and climbed back up again to 3000 feet.

"Okay," he said, "we'll try a spin to the left." Away we went again. I really got dizzy as we twirled downward. He landed the plane and suggested that I take over in the pilot's left hand seat and he would sit in the co-pilot's seat on the right. Up we climbed to 3000 feet. That was easy enough. "Now," he said, "try a spin to the left." I did what I thought I should, but man oh man, my stomach seemed to come up into my mouth and before I knew it, I vomited. It's a good thing that I managed to open the window, but what a mess on the outside of that plane.

So we landed, since you can't learn too much when you are sick. My instructor said to come back the following morning and we'd try again. The next two mornings the weather was not flyable at all. On Thursday night, my instructor said, "You had better be here at daybreak and we'll get some spins in before the inspector comes tomorrow morning at eleven o'clock.

31

The inspector arrived. I asked the instructor what I should do. "Oh," he said, "you can do it all right. It's too bad the weather was bad and we couldn't get more flying time in, but you can do it I'm sure. Just take off and climb to 3000 feet and bring the plane to a stall, then full left rudder and full left and full back on the stick - spin down to 1000 feet and do the opposite to recover. But don't you tell the inspector that you haven't had the training." Oh, Oh, now what should I do? I prayed silently for the Lord to help me.

The Inspector came over and said, "Ready?" I said, "Okay."

"Climb to 3000 feet, right over there," pointing in a westerly direction. "Make two spins to the left and two to the right. Leave your engine idling and come in for a landing."

I climbed into the plane with fear and trembling. I started the engine, rolled down the runway and took off, I climbed to 3000 feet, praying all the way. Now, I tried to bring the plane to a stall, but seemingly it didn't want to stall. I pushed full left rudder and full back on the stick and full to the left. We fell over the left wing, the plane began to circle - tighter and tighter as we spiralled earthward. I didn't like it at all. I began to feel nauseated. I didn't blackout, but I did "greyout". I couldn't see a thing, everything was a dull grey as we spiralled faster and faster downward. I knew this was no spin and I knew I must pull out of it quickly. The Lord helped me as I reversed the proceedings and you can imagine how glad I was as the plane recovered to level flight - less than 500 feet above the ground.

I climbed back up to 3000 feet. I tried another spin to the left and about the same thing happened. I didn't like it at all. The next try was one to the right and that was about as bad as the other. By this time I felt like a rag. I was completely exhausted - that was enough for me, so I landed.

The inspector came over and said, "Do you call those spins? - that will never do. I have other students to test and if you wish to try again later, let me know."

Well, I did feel bad, even though I couldn't tell the inspector that I didn't have the training for spins. I went over to a hamburg stand and had coffee and a hamburg and felt better. I watched the other students fly up to 3000 feet, spin the plane

32

left and right. I observed exactly what the plane was doing. When the inspector tested his last student he asked if I wanted to try again.

I said I would.

"This time fly over there," as he pointed in an easterly direction. I really prayed as I climbed up to 3000 feet. This time I brought the plane to a complete stall and over it went in what I thought was a pretty good left hand spin. I recovered and climbed back up to 3000 feet and wonder of wonders, the plane did about exactly what I wanted it to do. I then made two spins to the right, let the engine idle and made a perfect landing. I taxied up to the inspector and he was all smiles. "Well," he said, "the last three attempts were perfect spins, so you get your licence." Boy, was I glad to hear him say that.

When I returned home war in Korea was not too good and mention was made in the papers about restricting imports from the States. I told my wife perhaps we had better put our order in for the new plane. We prayed about it, then I sent a telegram to get the plane ready. Within three and a half weeks a telegram came back - "Your plane is ready for delivery, come down and get it." Now different individuals and churches had sent funds in marked "for the plane." All these went into the bank and when the telegram arrived, I went to the bank to find I had a total of $465.00. I remembered I had promised to pay cash and also that the plane would cost nearly $7,000. Here I was with only $465.00, now what?

That was August 28, 1950 - the Canadian National Railway was on strike, so no CNR trains were operating; there was no bus service out of Hearst and I couldn't take my car because how could I bring both the car and the plane back?

I took my $465. and scurried about town into the different stores looking for a travelling commercial salesman. At last I was rewarded - this salesman said he was leaving for Toronto in fifteen minutes and he would be glad to have my company, especially since I could do some of the driving.

I hurried home, got a few things ready and was back in less than fifteen minutes. Our drive to Toronto was uneventful. He dropped me off and drove on. I stood there thinking, now what? People were hurrying to work in the morning hour. I saw a man coming towards me whom I recognized as belonging to one of our big churches in Toronto. Was I ever glad to see him.

We shook hands and he asked what I was doing in Toronto.

I said, "I'm on my way to Lock Haven, Penna. to get my new plane for the missionary work in the North."

"Oh," he said, "that's wonderful. We've been praying for you and we are interested in what you are doing."

That sounded good to me, and I thought right now would be a good time to put in a little word, so I said, "I appreciate your interest and prayers. I already have $465.00 towards the plane and if you people would like to help that would be fine."

"But," he said, "I didn't mean it that way." Talk about a person's heart dropping to the ground - well that's exactly how I felt when he said that, and he just let it sink in too. It seemed we just stood there silently for a long time, but I don't suppose it was more than a minute.

Then he said, "John, we have watched you, we have seen how God's hand is upon your life. We have prayed for you and we have already had a business meeting at our church and have decided that when you are ready to buy that plane, our church will buy it for you and we don't need help from anyone else."

"Well, praise the Lord. I could hardly believe it. I was soon on my way to Lock Haven and paid cash for the plane. We do serve the wonderful Lord! That man's name was Alf Huntley of the Stone Church, Toronto, Ontario, Canada.

That first plane was a Piper Super Cub - the largest and most powerful cub, Piper had made up to that time. Now I was ready and prepared to take the Gospel to the far North.

I ordered and received quite a number of aeronautical maps of the northland which I studied carefully. I noticed on some were blank places, marked 'unmapped', which I soon found out were only too true. I gathered supplies together for a survival kit. This included dehydrated foods, tea, sugar, powdered milk, a tent, sleeping bag, axe, hatchet, rabbit snare wire, fishing lines, hooks and lures, shotgun, snowshoes, a blow pot to preheat the engine, and an engine tent as the temperature often dropped to 40-50 degrees, below zero Fahrenheit and even colder.

CHAPTER 4

INTO THE UNKNOWN NORTH

"And they shall come from . . . the north . . . and shall sit down in the Kingdom of God." Luke 13: 29

I remember my first long flight into the unknown north. I loaded the plane, preheated the engine and as I took off and climbed upward over Johnson Lake, just north of Hearst, strange thoughts entered my mind. "Will I ever be back here again?" Tears flowed down my cheeks as I thought of leaving my wife and family, - perhaps for the last time. It would not have taken too much to have changed my mind. But the great commission of Jesus prevailed, "Go ye into all the world and preach the Gospel," so I kept on going.

I planned my flight route to stop at many Indian settlements along the way. I continued until I reached the barren lands of the far north, where it is too cold for trees to grow, and where there would be Eskimo settlements.

God blessed my ministry among the Indian people. I found them very interested in the truths of God's Word. Many responded to the invitation to accept Christ as Saviour. As I preached in English an interpreter translated the message into the local language.

I continued flying north day after day. After leaving the James Bay area, visiting the settlements along the eastern shore, I flew on north into the Hudson Bay area. This is a rugged part of the country with many high jagged hills. This one afternoon March 6, 1951 I found myself flying between Great Whale River and Richmond Gulf. I wanted to reach Richmond Gulf before dark, but as I flew north alone in my little Piper Super cub, I realized that I was battling against a very strong head wind. At times it was so strong that I hardly made any headway at all. Time was running out and sure enough the sun disappeared below the horizon of the Hudson Bay on my left. One by one I saw the little stars begin to appear and all this time the winds were just howling. As darkness settled down, I was still many many miles from my destination, up at 4000 feet and no place to land below in the rugged terrain.

All at once the realization of the danger I was in, gripped my heart. A tremendous flood of fear overwhelmed me and I was afraid that this was it - I felt I would never survive the predicament I was in. Darkness all around me and facing a howling headwind, I do not know just how long this great fear gripped my heart. But suddenly, the presence of the Lord filled my heart in that little plane. The Lord took away all my fear and gave me joy and gladness. I began to sing "Under the blood of Jesus, safe in the Shepherd's fold, under the blood of Jesus, safe while the ages roll; Safe though the worlds may crumble, safe though the stars grow dim; under the blood of Jesus, I am secure in Him."

I realized that someone, someplace was praying for me, maybe it was my wife. God answered that prayer and although the outward circumstances were worse than ever and deteriorating, I had God's peace in my heart and I was not afraid any longer.

I continued flying north, toward, where the map showed was the settlement of Richmond Gulf, on an island. Even though it was now night, and darkness had settled down, still I was able to know my location because of the snow on the ground and I could make out the different rivers as they emptied into Hudson Bay.

At long last I found the island which, according to my map, was where Richmond Gulf Village should be. I circled and circled and circled that island many times trying to see a light or even a building, but I couldn't see any sign of life at all. Then I thought I must be mistaken, so I flew in wider circles trying my best to find this settlement. At last I looked away off into the east and I thought for sure that I could see a flicker of a light. I turned the plane into that direction and flew for quite some time until I saw the flicker of light again and sure enough as I flew closer, I made out the shapes of buildings and even people running around on the snow-covered ground. Was I ever glad to see human life again!

Now, if I could only get down to terra firma all would be well. I knew that even with my limited experience, that there were high hammocks of ice pushed up by the tide waters and if I hit one of these in landing all would be over. I really prayed for God's help as I came down for a landing. It was very hard to see just where that surface was but at last I felt the skis touch and I pulled back on the throttle and the plane settled down.

Whew! Solid earth again! Was I ever glad to be down as Eskimos and a white fur trader came out to greet me. The fur trader invited me to stay with him and his wife and I sure appreciated their kindness. Before going to bed he told me of an Eskimo brought into the settlement from many miles away who was very sick and near death, and he wondered if I could fly him out to a hospital. I promised to try in the morning if the weather permitted. Next morning, the wind was howling louder than ever - we knew that a storm was not far behind. After breakfast, we loaded the Eskimo lad and his mother into the back seat of the plane. I had a few Eskimos hang on to each wing as I taxied out on the ice for a take off. I told them to hang on tight and not let go till I gave the signal because that plane would have been blown across the ice and smashed to pieces. I told them that I would try to fly south to a hospital if possible, but in case I had to turn back, they were to come out on the ice and divide into two parties. I would fly between them and cut the engine while they grabbed the wings of the plane before the wind had a chance to blow us over.

I revved the engine up to full throttle, the plane vibrated hard. I gave the Eskimos the "let go" signal and that plane rose almost vertically. I circled around and headed south. I could see a great storm wall about 35-40 miles away, right in our path. I tried to fly under it, but the storm was down to the ground; I flew east, but couldn't see any opening; I flew west, but all in vain. At last I had to make the decision to turn back. What else could I do? It would have been suicide to try and fly into that storm.

After what seemed hours, we again reached the settlement. As I circled I was glad to see the Eskimos run out on the ice as I had informed them. The plane settled down to just above the ice and I flew in between the two groups of Eskimos. I cut the engine and they grabbed the wings and we were safe. Thank the Lord!

The storm reached the settlement before nightfall. Winds were terrific and the blinding snow cut visibility to zero. That night the Eskimo lad died. A number of the Eskimos came and requested that I conduct the funeral service.

I had held a few services already for these dear people and they responded to the Gospel message and some had prayed to the Lord to save them.

There was another mission located here and when I visited the personnel, I felt quite a hostility, but nothing was actually said to cause alarm.

The storm lasted for five days. On the fourth day, I went out for a walk up the hill north of the settlement. I found hundreds of ptarmigan — a partridge - like white bird which the Eskimo hunted. They were very tame and allowed me to get within a few feet of them before they hopped away.

While walking away from the village, I looked back to see if I could still see the buildings, as the storm was gradually abating. After going north for quite a distance I walked back toward the settlement. Then I took a notion to walk west out on the ice of Richmond Gulf, periodically looking back to see the buildings as I did not want to lose sight of them. I returned to the fur trader's home, but before going in I decided to take a little walk east. After going for some distance I turned to see if I could still see the buildings.

As I glanced across the landscape I noticed the door of the mission open and a figure dressed in black came out, crouching low to the ground as he approached me. I didn't like the looks of things, but decided to walk a bit further. He kept following, not standing up, but still crouching. I thought I had better not go too far and decided to make a circle and return.

While making the circle, and keeping my eyes on the crouching figure, he stopped, but I continued. A shot rang out and at that same instant, I heard the whine of the bullet. The crouching figure sprang erect and ran back into the mission building. I thanked God that I was not hit, but I really was trembling all over.

On the fifth day the storm calmed down enough for me to fly on northward until I reached Port Harrison on March 12, 1951. Here they had a two-way radio and a Department of Transport weather station. I sent a message across Hudson Bay to Churchill, Manitoba and on to my wife at Hearst, Ontario.

Little did I realize what was happening on the "outside". While stranded for five days at Richmond Gulf someone started the story that I had crashed and was killed. The newspapers printed articles about it, the radio broadcasted the news. My brothers and sisters in southern Ontario heard and read about it and phoned or wired my wife to inquire about the accident. Other friends in the States heard about it and phoned and telegrammed as well as sent letters of sympathy to my wife.

At first she didn't believe the story could be true, but after so many calls of sympathy, she thought, "Is it true?" She tried to conduct a children's service in the church, but a deep depression made it impossible for her to continue, so she asked Rose, our oldest daughter, still so very young, to carry on and she went into the bedroom to pray.

She prayed, "Lord, have you taken my husband and left me with four small children?" The burden was extremely heavy as she tried to pray. Then all at once, she received the assurance that I was all right. Immediately she felt refreshed and went back to continue the service.

The next day while attending a parents' night at the school, many of the people came over to sympathize with her but she insisted she did not believe the story of the plane crash and that I was all right. Some people thought she was queer. Then my radio message arrived and you can imagine her delight when she received it. Yes God is good to all who will put their trust in Him.

FOOD FOR THE BODY

Spillenaar family out hunting partridge and rabbits.

PLANES AND INCIDENTS

Rev. John Spillenaar in Aeronautical training at Moody
Bible Inst., Chicago, Ill.

Our first plane with the congregation at Haileybury, Ontario.

The first plane, a Piper PA18 after the tide and storm broke it loose and carried it over a mile up the river. We found it sitting on an island sixty feet from the water, with **no damage.**

After our first plane burnt inside the hangar at Johnson Lake, Hearst, Ontario.

Rev. George Upton of the National office and myself taking delivery of our second plane, a 170 Cessna.

Our second plane, a 170 Cessna at Fort Severn with Bob Jones on the left who came to help build a church, missionaries Grace Oates and Ruth Anotonelli and myself.

CF-JAY, our third plane and the Spillenaar Family. Left to right, John, Tyyne, Daniel, David, Rose and Grace.

CF-JAY after a severe storm at Porcupine Lake, South Porcupine.

Refueling our fourth plane, CF LGT somewhere in the north.

Our fourth plane, a 180 Cessna.

Our fifth plane, a 185 Cessna which is still in operation.

CHAPTER 5

MY FIRST GLIMPSE OF ESKIMO IGLOOS
"Lift up your eyes, and look on the fields; for they are white already to harvest." Jn 4: 35B

After leaving the village of Richmond Gulf enroute to Port Harrison, a distance of approximately 190 miles, I flew along the coast line of Hudson Bay. The weather had been good, but soon deteriorated, and I found myself flying into a snowstorm. At first the visibility wasn't too bad, especially when I descended to about 100 feet above the ice of Hudson Bay, but I had to keep a careful watch for islands which arose sometime 200 feet above the ice.

As I flew on, the storm increased, which made visibility quite bad. I decided to find some place to land, so I throttled back, pulled on twenty degrees of flap and tried to see how smooth the ice surface was below me.

All at once I saw what appeared to be many heaps of snow, but no, there were people crawling out of them, so they must be Igloos. How thankful I was that I had not tried to land there. I pulled up higher and was able to keep going till I reached Port Harrison.

The Lord enabled me to visit many of our northern settlements and conduct services in each of them during the winter and summer of 1951. On August 20th, 1951 I reached York Factory, Manitoba, on the Hayes River where it empties into Hudson Bay. This was my first visit to this settlement. The Hudson Bay Co. manager was Jock Halliday, a very fine, hospitable man. He invited me for supper and to spend the night with him. The service was held in the school room which was packed with eager listeners.

Next morning I heard Jock preparing breakfast, so I got up,

47

and went into the kitchen. Jock said that breakfast would be ready in about fifteen minutes. That would give me time enough to go down and get some things out of the plane which we had tied down the night before.

But Jock said, "No, don't go down now. I'll go with you after breakfast." I wondered at the time about this but didn't say anything. After a good hearty breakfast we washed the dishes.

Then he said, "Let's go down to the plane." Out we went and walked to the river's edge and looked down over the high embankment to where we had tied the plane. No plane was there! Just an empty place! I was dumbfounded. I couldn't even speak for quite a while. Here I was, away up at York Factory, and my plane was gone! Jock knew about this, as some of the Indians had reported it to him, before I got up, and that's why he stopped me before breakfast.

While we were standing there, a canoe with two men came down the river. They called something in Cree which I could not understand. Then Jock said, "I don't believe it. I just don't believe it."

I said, "Jock, what don't you believe?"

He said, "These men say that there is a small plane sitting on an island over a mile up the river - but I don't believe it."

"Well," I said, "The least we can do is to go upriver to see."

"O.K," Jock said. "I'll send my clerk with you in our Hudson Bay Co. boat with an outboard motor."

In just a few minutes we were on our way. Sure enough, there was my missionary plane, sitting on an island, over a mile upriver from where we had tied it down. The ropes were dangling from the wing struts and the plane was approximately sixty feet up on the island from the water's edge. Was I ever glad to see that plane - especially that it was safe and sound without a damaged mark on it.

We returned to the village and told Jock Halliday about it. He was surprised and excited as he told me what likely happened. During the previous night the tide was extra high because of a strong wind blowing off the Hudson Bay. We tied the plane up when the tide was about half way. Then when the extra high tide came in, the water lifted the plane, which pulled the stakes out of the ground and the tide water flowing upriver carried the plane with it. It could have gone seven or eight miles upriver before stopping. But then when the tide went out, the plane floated downstream toward Hudson Bay. I am sure that God directed that plane to land on the Island and be safe - rather than be carried out to Hudson Bay and be lost.

Jock said, "Take shovels, crowbars and a few men and go back and see if you can get the plane into the water."

There were huge boulders between the plane and the water, which we had to roll out of the way. We then dug trenches in the gravel for the pontoons to fit into. While we worked the tide was returning and the water was rising. But this tide was not as high as the previous one. We waited till the water reached the highest point - then it began to recede. We tied ropes on the front of the pontoons, so one man pulled on each rope while others pushed from behind, and I was inside with the engine running. Gradually the plane moved forward on the gravel till we reached the water. At last the plane was in deep enough water to float and were we glad that it was not damaged. We do thank God for this another miracle.

CHAPTER 6

MY FIRST ENGINE FAILURE
"He shall call upon me, and I will answer him, I will be with him in trouble, I will deliver him and honour him." Psalm 91: 15.

All through the month of January 1952, I visited many villages including Sioux Lookout, Dog Hole, Pickle Lake, Caribou Lake, Osnaburg House, Big Beaverhouse, Big Trout Lake, Bearskin, Sanchigo, Shamattawa, and many more places.

On another occasion I was flying alone from village to village conducting services, leaving Bibles, New Testaments and tracts in their language and even clothing for them to wear. I would arrive at a settlement perhaps at ten o'clock in the morning and people would gather around in curiosity. The first thing I did was to shake hands with them and try to find an interpreter. The Hudson Bay Fur Trading Company usually had a trading post in each of these settlements and they always had an interpreter who spoke English as well as the native language. Within a few minutes, we would be gathered in one of the larger teepees, tent or a log home for a Gospel service.

I found people very responsive to the Gospel message. They listened very attentively to the Word of God as it was being interpreted by one of their own people. I explained to them in simple language that the Bible said, "All have sinned and come short of the glory of God." And that Jesus died on the Cross of Calvary to save everyone from their sins; but that each one must voluntarily accept Jesus Christ as Saviour and Lord if they wanted to become true "born again" believers, in the family of God.

At the end of each service the people were given an opportunity to make a decision for Christ. In most of the services it was a great joy to see men, women and young people come forward, many with tears running down their faces, to accept Jesus into their hearts and lives.

What a joy it was for me to listen to their testimonies which were interpreted into English for me. A summary of the average testimony would be like this: "I have lived here in this village all my life. All of you people know me. I have always attended church services and took for granted that I was on my way to Heaven; but when Mr. Spillenaar came and explained to us from the Word of God that we were all sinners and that we all needed to be saved from our sins through the precious Blood of Jesus, I then realized that I too needed Jesus. Now I have prayed and asked Jesus to come into my heart. He has come in, and I just feel so wonderful. I know now for sure that I am a child of God."

They appreciated these services so very much and tried their best to thank me. They always wanted me to have a meal with them - no matter what time of day it was and I enjoyed many meals with these precious people. After a meal, I would bid them farewell as I climbed into the plane which was christened "Wings of the Gospel". And away to another settlement, another service and to another meal, then off again to reach another village before dark - on and on - day after day.

This one particular morning, February 29, 1952 I was at Ogoki in Northern Ontario and the sun was shining brightly as I prepared our missionary plane for a flight to the next Indian village. I noticed that it was thirty two degrees fahrenheit below zero, as I swept the heavy frost off the wings and tail. At times the frost stuck so fast to the wings that I had to "see saw" a rope, back and forth, by standing behind the wing and throwing a rope up and over the leading edge and bringing the two ends back behind. I pulled the rope on top back toward me, giving slack on the lower rope, then pulling on the lower rope, slacking the upper rope and working away from the base of the wing next to the fuselage out to the tip and back again until all the frost was loosened.

Next I prepared the engine tent, which fitted over the engine cowling and down to the ground. I got under this tent with my blow pot, which is like a blow torch using non leaded naphtha gasoline. I pumped air into the gas tank of this blow pot until the pressure was built up sufficiently, then lit it. This blow pot throws a terrific heat and one must be very careful as there is always gasoline and oil around. I always stayed inside the tent with the blow pot until the engine was warm enough to start.

I heard of one pilot who wanted to do two jobs at once; so he lit the blow pot under his plane engine tent, then went out to sweep the snow off the wings. Suddenly he saw smoke and flames envelope the plane engine and in just moments he had no more plane. I timed my preheating the engine according to temperature and winds. If the wind was calm it usually took one minute of heat for each degree below zero, thus thirty-two degrees below zero, I would figure on preheating about thirty-two minutes. But if the wind was blowing, it could take a few more minutes of preheat. Completing this, I would remove the engine tent and turn the propeller many times by hand to loosen the oil inside the engine. I then would get in the cockpit, prime the engine with three and four pushes on the primer, crack the throttle about one half an inch, and press the starter button. Usually the plane started without any further trouble but sometimes if the battery was low or if it was extra cold like fifty to sixty degrees below zero, I had to swing the propeller with the switch on contact until it started. I always let the engine idle slowly until the instruments indicated normal heat, then I was ready for take-off. In the extremely cold winter months I would remove the battery the night before and take it inside a home to keep it warm.

This particular morning, I plotted my course in a direct line to the next village. Taking off, I climbed to two thousand feet and headed in the right direction. It was a beautiful morning with the sun shining brightly and not a cloud in the sky. I looked over the side of the plane and noticed a small herd of caribou in a clearing below, pawing away the snow to eat the moss which they feed on. Sometime later I noticed another small herd of about two dozen caribou. I thought to myself that at least a person would have meat to eat if for some reason he had to crash land. Little did I realize that I would soon be down there.

I was enjoying the flight immensely; the presence of the Lord was so real and it was such a beautiful day. Then all of a sudden, without warning, the plane engine stopped and the

52

propeller stood still. My natural reaction would be to panic and do the wrong thing. But in a flash, I called upon the Lord to help me and that verse of scripture immediately came to my mind in Psalm 91: 15 - 16; that in a time of trouble if we call upon the Lord that He will hear me and answer me and deliver me. I cried, "Lord, that's your Holy Word, which cannot fail. You promised to deliver me, because I am in trouble for sure. And I call upon you to help me and I'm standing on your promise that somehow you will deliver me."

All this happened so quickly, but now I felt the assurance that the Lord somehow would help me. The plane was going down; but the Lord gave me presence of mind to keep the control stick forward so that the plane would be able to glide and maintain flying speed. One can hold the stick back to keep the plane level for a short while without stalling and going out of control into a spin and crash. As the plane glided down, I was able to turn and manouvre the plane looking for a place to land. No river, lake or clearing was in sight. All I could see was heavy bush country of tall spruce trees. It looked as if I would have to crash land into the trees. On the way down, I checked and found I had plenty of gas and everything appeared to be in good flying condition. I even tried to start the engine by pressing the starter button, but with no response.

By this time I was nearing the trees, when I saw a very small opening, which looked about the size of a saucer. I realized this was the only place to put the plane down. I really prayed for the Lord to help, because everything had to be just right. If I approached this little clearing too high or too fast, I would hit the trees on the other side. If too low or too slow, I would hit the trees on this side. I knew I didn't have a choice. But praise the Lord, I missed the trees on this side and landed in the centre of this little patch. The snow was deep - five or six feet - and when the plane stopped, the engine was buried in the snow and the tail in the air at an angle of about forty five degrees.

How glad I was to be safe and I held a thanksgiving service right there. I prayed, "Thank you Lord that I am safe and not hurt and that the plane is not damaged; thank you for a safe landing."

Then as I realized just where I was and how would I ever get out of here, some of my joy disappeared. What could I do now? I opened the door, removed my seat belt and with my shovel and snowshoes, got out to survey my situation. It didn't look too good. I wondered why the engine quit in the first place. I shovelled all the snow away from the engine and propeller, which had not touched the ground and was in perfect condition. Opening the engine cowling, it did not take long to find the problem and fix it. I climbed back in the plane, pulled the shovel and snowshoes in after me, shut the door, tightened my seat belt and pressed the starter.

The engine started just like it should and sounded good. But now what? What can I do to get out of this small clearing? The plane skis were deep down in the snow and the plane itself was pointed down rather than up.

I began to pray again. "Lord it was a great miracle to get me here safe and I thank you for it; but now it's going to take a greater miracle to get me out of here. I don't see how we can get out, but please help me." I thought to myself if there were two of us, we could go into the bush, cut down some trees and make blocks of wood. Then one could lift up on one wing a little and the other could put a block of wood under the one ski and then go to the other side and do the same, and back and forth until the plane would at least be on the level instead of nosing down. What could I do alone? Nothing like that. But I could pray, which I did. I just sat there, with the engine running full throttle and while I prayed I looked around, and then I felt a little tremor go through the plane. Then it began to vibrate just a little at first and then harder and harder until now it was really shaking.

I've thought since, "Isn't this the way we all get some time -- stuck in a rut and heading in the wrong direction spiritually, and we need the Lord to give us a good shaking to loosen us up and get us going upward again."

The Lord really shook that plane; then it began to move. It climbed up out of the snow till it was level; then it began to move forward. But the trees were just ahead; I did not want to hit them and damage the plane. Oh, I thought, if I can just swing around in a circle and come back on my same tracks and go faster and faster in this circle, I will gain speed and try to fly up out of here. So I tried to swing around but there was no room even to make one circle in that deep snow. One hasn't all day to think about things, as they happen so quickly; but I knew I had to do one of two things. Turn the key to shut the engine off before I hit the trees because a plane on skis has no brakes, that meant I would have to stay there, which I didn't want to do. Or else try to fly up and over the trees. But a plane must have flying speed in order to fly, let alone climb, and there we were moving slowly, with the trees getting closer and closer. I prayed again, "Lord, if any one ever needed help, I need your help now, please Lord help me to get out of here." And while I prayed, I pulled back on the flap control with one hand and pulled back on the stick control with the other hand and the plane started up into the air just like a helicopter, I was so amazed I held my breath, as if that would help matters. We reached the top of the trees and levelled out and away. Man, was I ever glad to get out of there. Yes, we serve a God of miracles. Our God is the same as the God of Moses, of Joshua, of David and Daniel and all the Old Testament prophets. He is the same yesterday, today, and forever!

April the 8th, 1952 was a great day for this Northland Missionary work. Our first two missionaries arrived: Miss Grace Oates from England and Miss Ruth Antonelli from St. Catharines, Ontario. I had had the opportunity of speaking and showing pictures of the Northland in various churches in Southern Ontario and had made an appeal for help, not only for finances to carry on, but also for personnel to come north to preach the Gospel. These two ladies volunteered to come - and now they had arrived at our home in Hearst, Ontario enroute to Fort Severn on the Hudson Bay. On April 9th we purchased supplies, loaded and refuelled the plane. Then on April 10th Grace Oates and I flew to Fort Severn via Nakina where we landed and refuelled - a distance of approximately five hundred and seventy miles. Since my plane was only a two seater, I had to take them in one at a time. It was a lovely day and we had a very good flight arriving at Fort Severn that same evening. The weather continued to be good so I flew south alone on April 11th and arrived home via Nakina that afternoon. We had time to refuel and load up the plane that evening for our next flight. April 12th was a nice day at Hearst so I flew back to Fort Severn with Ruth Antonelli. The last one hundred and fifty miles was through quite a snow storm and we were indeed glad to at last see the village of Fort Severn.

Spring breakup would usually come anytime between April 15th to May 1st, at which time we would remove the skis and install the pontoons for summer operations. It was during the spring breakup period and the fall freeze up period that I would go south to hold missionary services in many churches. The people would respond and were glad to donate funds in missionary offerings to pay for this operation in the north.

Being appointed director of the northern area from North Bay on April 4th, 1952, I felt a concern that we ought to have a camp meeting where people could come from all over the north to enjoy at least two weeks of Camp. Our Western District Superintendent, Rev. J.H. Blair of Hamilton, Ontario encouraged us to purchase a property. It was on July 20th, 1952 that our Silver Birches Camp opened on the shores of Round Lake just south of Kirkland Lake. This Camp has been a great blessing to hundreds of people.

During the summer months I was able to fly all through northern Ontario and into northern Manitoba as far north as Churchill, Manitoba on the Hudson Bay where we arrived on August 15th, 1952. I had Rev. Gordon McElhoes, pastor of the church at Parry Sound, Ontario, with me. We left Hearst on August 12th and visited at Fort Albany and Attawapiskat on James Bay - then on north to Sutton Lake, then Winisk and Fort Severn on Hudson Bay. Then we flew into Manitoba to York Factory and had services in all these places. Some of these were held in the mornings, others in the afternoon or evening - whenever we arrived.

Between York Factory and Churchill we flew into very bad weather. At first it was a cold sleeting rain which turned to a driving soft snow. Visibility was getting very poor so I decided to try and find a landing place as daylight was also running out. I couldn't find a lake to land on and the rivers inland were narrow and rocky, so I flew east toward Hudson Bay and noticed the Broad River which appeared to be suitable. We made a good landing and tied the plane to some small willow bushes on the river bank. Through the driving snow, I noticed what appeared to be a shack not too far east of us toward the Bay. On investigating later, we found that it had been built during the war years and was used as a lookout for enemy submarines. It leaked badly but we managed to huddle in, both of us in my large sleeping bag. It was quite an uncomfortable night, and we were glad to see the day dawn.

During the night the tide water went out, and we found the plane, still tied, both pontoons on the bottom of the dry river and sitting on a forty-five degree angle, one wing high in the air and the other away down. We managed to swing the plane around and get it into the water. We had no difficulty taking off as the weather was now good, and we flew into Churchill. On this visit we made preliminary arrangements to purchase property and open a church here.

It was very busy all that summer of 1952 - flying to the many villages and conducting services for the people. I remember one time after I had landed at a certain village, quite a crowd gathered around the plane and they wanted me to conduct a service for them. So I told them I would be ready in about one hours time. Then two men came up close to me and asked if I could perform marriages. I said that I could and asked who wanted to get married. It was this man who was asking the question through the interpreter. He asked if I would perform his wedding before the service. But I suggested that he wait till after the service - to which he agreed. I then asked him the necessary questions so that I could send a report to the Ontario Government. After getting all this information I needed about him, I asked what his intended wife's name was. "Oh," he said, "I don't know yet. I'll have to go and see." It was quite a laughable matter, but I dared not laugh nor show any amusement, as I could see that he was really in earnest. I suggested that perhaps he had better wait till morning, and that I would be ready to perform the marriage then if he so desired.

We had a very good service that evening after which I stayed at the Hudson Bay Manager's house. The next morning I went to the plane to get ready to fly out; and as I was refuelling, I noticed the same two men come toward me looking quite sad.

After awhile the man spoke up and said, "No wedding to-day."

I asked him, "What happened?"

He said, "No one wants to get married."

So that was the end of that episode. But I have performed many marriages, dedications of babies, and funerals all through the Northland.

On my last flight of the 1952 summer season, I flew a large plane load of supplies to the two missionaries at Fort Severn. I arrived there on September 24th. The weather was not too good for flying so I waited for better weather. Some of the Indian men and I went out and shot some big Canada geese. I also worked on the building where Grace and Ruth lived and held their services, to make it warmer for the cold winter months.

I stayed at the Hudson Bay Manager's home, Gordon Douglas. While we were eating breakfast on October 1st, we heard the wind just a-howling as a terrific wind storm came in. Just then an Indian rushed in - and was so excited as he hollered something about the plane.

Mr. Douglas and I rushed out and down to the river bank and there was my plane sailing - backward across the wide river. The wind had torn the plane loose. The ropes had broken. And there it was - driven by approximately sixty to seventy mile winds. What could we do? Some of the Indians said they could go out in their canoes and see if they could catch the plane. I said, "No, don't go. It would be suicide to go. You'll drown!" But they would not listen. Two men each in two canoes started to cross the river. The waves were high and as we watched the plane being tossed about, it appeared as if it may go under at any moment. The Indian men in the canoes got to the plane but it was impossible to tow it back against the wind so they went on past the plane and onto an Island which lay in its path. They waited till the plane reached the Island and got a hold of the tail and lifted the plane up till the wind had pushed it high and dry on this Island. The Indians tied it down and it stayed there all that day and night till the next day when the wind had subsided and I was able to go over and bring it back. It was not damaged and I was able to fly out that day.

After freeze up time, I wanted to fly another load of supplies up to Fort Severn, as Grace and Ruth, the missionaries, had written a long list of needs - and I was anxious to deliver them. The lakes and rivers in the Hearst area appeared to be quite safe around Christmas time, but I wondered what the conditions were like at Fort Severn. Radio communications were out, so there was nothing to do but try. On December 29, 1952, I left Hearst and flew north to Fort Severn. Head winds delayed my arrival at the village till darkness was beginning to settle in. I circled around, but it was difficult to see how rough the marked out runway on the river was. As I touched down, I realized it was very rough and the plane bounced along until the undercarriage gave way and allowed the skis to spread outward. This brought the propeller in contact with the snow and ice, and the right wing up also hit the surface. At last the plane came to a stop, and I got out and surveyed the damage. The wing tip was not too badly damaged except for the fabric, but the two blades of the metal propeller were badly bent and the undercarriage broken. Many of the folk at the village came down as we unloaded the plane and left it for the night.

Next morning the Catholic Priest, Rev. Morin and I went to the plane to see if we might be able to repair it enough for me to fly it out empty. He had some half inch galvanized water pipe which we took down and some blocks of wood and heavy wire. First we raised the plane into the proper position and set it on the blocks of wood. We then drew the broken undercarriage back into place, and with lengths of the water pipe, we wired the undercarriage into position. We tested it by raising and lowering the wings which brought stress to bear on the undercarriage. It stood up well and I could manage that part of it. We got the Indian women to make a canvas cover to fit over the end of the wing - to about three feet back. We laced it down tight and it looked fairly strong.

But what about the bent up propeller? I removed it and we carried it to the Catholic Mission workshop. It was warm there so we left the propeller overnight to bring it to room temperature all through. The next morning we began to straighten it. One of us would hold it at the proper angle while the other would strike it with a wooden mallet. This was a long and tedious task, but at last we had straightened out both blades - until it looked good to both of us. We installed it on the plane, preheated the engine, then fired up to see what would happen. Well - Praise the Lord - we were both delighted to see that the engine worked very good, with no propeller vibration.

I taxied around to test the undercarriage. All stood up well and I was ready to fly out as soon as the weather permitted. It was cold, working on that plane, right out in the open, with a strong wind blowing off Hudson Bay, and I was so grateful for the help of Rev. Morin. It took us three days to complete these emergency repairs and each night we held services. On January 1st, I performed tne marriage ceremony for Lazarus Stony and Modena Crowe. Then on January 2nd, 1953, I flew non-stop from Fort Severn to Hearst with a strong tail wind, in five hours and forty minutes. I was so glad to be back home again. After a few days at home, I flew the plane to Orillia Airways in Orillia, where Harry Stirk and his men made the proper repairs.

I had built a hangar for the plane just off shore in Johnsons Lake at Hearst, Ontario to remove the skis and install pontoons for summer. Inside the hangar we built a plank platform under each wing and left the centre open for the plane to rest on ice in winter or in the water on pontoons in the summer. We always backed the plane in.

I also maintained a supply of aviation gasoline in forty-five gallon drums. One of these was open and I had the pump inserted to refuel the plane. The hose was long enough to reach both wing tanks.

On May 6th, 1953, my youngest son, David who was five and a half years old had walked out the two miles with me -- from our home in Hearst to Johnsons Lake -- and he was playing around as I endeavoured to remove the skis. It is quite a job to do alone and I was having trouble removing one bolt. I thought if I heated that bolt with a blow torch it would come out easily. David was playing under the far wing and I had an uneasy feeling about him there. This hangar was covered with metal and the large front doors were shut. It was a nice warm spring day as the sun beat down on the metal.

I called David to come over and play on the side of the plane where I was working; and you know how boys are -- and girls are just the same; he just kept on playing over there. This uneasy feeling persisted and I called David to come and hand me a wrench -- more to get him over than to help, actually -- and he came.

I lit the blow torch and heated that bolt a little. Then I shut off the torch and tried to remove it.

It still would not come out. So I lit this torch again to heat the bolt better.

All of a sudden, the air just above me appeared to catch on fire. There was no explosion at first but just a flash fire in the air -- flames in the air -- then quickly it moved over to the wing and it started burning. I dropped the torch and grabbed the fire extinguisher and pumped a few times at the fire but soon realized it was no use. Grabbing David, we hurried outside the hangar. As we moved toward shore one gas tank exploded, then I heard my shot gun cartridges in my survival kit go off one by one. The other gas tank exploded. By this time David and I reached the shore and looked back. Black smoke poured out of the small door facing shore through which we had escaped. Then we heard a bigger explosion and I knew one of the forty-five gallon drums of gas exploded. The roof was torn open and smoke and flames belched skyward. Then another great explosion and another until all six drums had exploded. It was a terrible sight and you can imagine the feeling I had when I knew we had no more plane.

We returned the two miles home which now seemed like twenty, feeling terribly down hearted. I phoned long distance to Pastor Hugh McAlister at Stone Church, Toronto. I couldn't help but cry as I sobbed out what happened. Pastor McAlister tried to encourage me saying that somehow things would work out.

But to me it appeared as if we had come to the end of a dead end street -- up against a brick wall and no way to turn.

After a few days of prayer and waiting on the Lord and carrying on the services in the Hearst Church, I began to think that somehow we must go on -- we must get another plane. By now we had built a few missions in the James and Hudson Bay area as well as inland -- and we had workers there who had to be supplied. I went to Toronto and contacted our headquarters -- we reviewed the whole situation. If we were to get another plane we decided it should be bigger and possibly an all metal one. The Stone Church Pastor and congregation were willing to turn the insurance money over to us towards another plane, but we still needed many more thousands of dollars. I went from church to church and held missionary meetings and told of the need of buying this larger plane. By June 30, 1953, I was flying a brand new Cessna 170 plane - registered CF-HCO. This was a four place plane rather than a two place like the Piper Super Cub. We needed a larger lake to operate from, so on July 9th, 1953, we moved to South Porcupine, Ontario where there was a good seaplane base to operate from.

CHAPTER 7

BETWIX AND BETWEEN

"Where two or three are gathered together in my name, there I am in the midst of them." Matt. 18:20

In my travels through the north conducting Gospel services, I had many varied experiences.

I had called in at Big Trout Lake a number of times and found the people responsive to the Gospel message. Many attended the services and in one such meeting six big Indian men including the chief, came forward to accept Jesus as Saviour. I knew that a white missionary was resident here but he had always been away on my previous visits. But this time as I landed the plane, and the crowd of Indians gathered around I noticed a white man in clerical garb among them. I knew he must be the missionary. Sure enough, he was. He invited me for supper as it was now just before dark. His wife was away, so he was chief cook and bottle washer.

While we were eating supper, he told me of the many years of his ministry in the North. But he said, "The people now appear to be worse than when I first came."

I asked him what he meant by that.

"Well," he said, "I was always able to get a number of them to attend my services, but now it's so hard to get even a few to come to the service. I really don't know what's the matter with them."

Later we were talking about the existing conditions, when we heard a knock at the door. He called out in the native language "to come in". The door opened and the chief with an interpreter walked in and stood between us facing me. After a brief greeting he spoke to me through the interpreter.

"Will you please hold a service for us while you are here?"

Now that really put me on the spot. Here I was in this other

63

man's home. He had just been telling me that the people didn't care to attend services and they were asking me to hold a service for them. What should I do? I didn't hesitate long. As I began to think of the reason I was in the North -- was it not to hold services and to help these people find God?

I said, "Sure, I'll be glad to have a service. But the plane is loaded with supplies for Fort Severn on the Hudson Bay. If the weather continues favourable, I will fly on and deliver my load. On the return flight I will stop in for a service."

"That would be fine," the chief said, and he appeared satisfied. He bid us farewell and started out. Just before disappearing in the night, he turned back and through his interpreter said, "Suppose the weather is bad in the morning and you cannot fly?"

I said, "If the weather is bad we'll have a service early tomorrow morning." He smiled and went on his way. The weather had been very good and even now the stars were shining brightly. But at daybreak next morning it was snowing and blowing -- no flying in that kind of weather.

While eating breakfast, my missionary friend expressed surprise at the chief's request.

He said, "It's hard to understand them. Just because you are here they ask for a service. Oh there may be five or six of them come, if that many."

As I looked out of the window while eating breakfast, I could see one's and two's and three's going through the storm toward the church building.

After washing the dishes my friend said, "Well, we may as well go over and see what's doing."

On our way over, no one was in sight, as it was so early in the morning and I wondered if my friend was right. We arrived at the church and he opened the door. I was close behind him. When he saw the place packed full with people he exclaimed, "Well, look at that!" and he almost fell backward over me.

I made my way to the platform and asked him if he would interpret for me. He agreed. We had a good song service and the Holy Spirit was present in a real way. The Lord gave me great liberty in proclaiming the Gospel story.

At the end of my sermon I said, "Now if any of you people

want to be saved, if you want to be ready for Heaven, you come up and we will pray for you.''

Somehow I felt that I wasn't getting the message across, so I asked my friend if he was telling the people exactly what I was telling him. He replied, "What do you mean to be saved? Do you mean they have to belong to your church?''

I said, "Listen here, I don't care what church they belong to. In fact they could belong to all churches and still go to Hell. They must belong to the Lord Jesus Christ.''

"Oh," he said, "that's different." He then told the people what I had said. Immediately I sensed a response, and I invited those to come up who really wanted to be saved. The whole congregation rose up and tried to come forward -- except two men in the back seat. One was a cripple and the other had carried him to the service.

You should have seen those people on their knees calling upon the Lord to save them. My missionary friend was so excited and said, "I've never seen anything like this in all my life.''

I replied, "That's the work of the Holy Spirit.''

On another flight, I called at a settlement. After a very good service in which many people came forward to accept the Lord as Saviour, the chief came to me and said, "I want you to promise me that you will take this message to all my people.''

"Well," I thought, "there are a lot of Indians in Canada and can I promise to take the Gospel to them all?'' While I was musing, he was waiting for my answer.

"Oh", I said, "I don't know where all your people live.''

He replied, "I will show you.'' We were talking through an interpreter.

Next morning when I arrived to prepare the plane for flight, there was the chief waiting at the plane, with a little knapsack in his hand. He was going to show me where his people lived.

He climbed into the rear seat of that Piper Super Cub and I climbed in the front seat and off we went. Once in a while he reached over and pointed either to the left or right for me to steer that way. After awhile he poked me in the back. I turned as much as possible and saw that he was pointing straight down. Sure enough, down among the thick forest, on the shore of a lake, I made out some log buildings and tents. We circled down and landed. The people were overjoyed to see us. They were so excited to see their chief and I, and talked so fast in their own language. The chief was telling them about me and the services. Pretty soon one left the group on the run and returned with a person who could speak a bit of English. He understood it better than he spoke. We were soon seated in one of the larger homes in a service. The people were packed in like sardines and I could see the earnest appealing look on their faces as the good news was told to them. After service the chief and the interpreter came to me and inquired, "Eat now?" But it was still early in the day so I said, "Let's keep going. It's too early to eat."

So off we flew again. With the same kind of direction finding we located another settlement which was not on my map. We landed and the same situation repeated itself. Again the request was made. "Eat now?" But still I didn't feel that hungry and as long as the weather was good I didn't want to waste time to eat, but wanted to reach as many of the people as we possibly could. Away we went. After the fourth meeting in four different places, darkness was beginning to settle down. Then we could not fly on, so when the chief came with his question, "Eat now?" I said, "O.K." You should have seen the big smile that came over his face. He spoke to our host. They hustled around and within a very short time, had what I would call a "cariboo stew", ready for us. They brought two big bowls, one for the chief and one for me. I looked at mine and with my spoon I pulled the cariboo hair to one side so it clung to the side of the bowl. Then I was able to eat. It was good. The chief, I noticed, didn't take time to separate the hair from the meat. He was as hungry as a bear and he soon gulped all his food down. Oh well, what are a few hairs?

Another episode I encountered was way up North. Airplane gasoline was hard to get and at this time I didn't have my own cache of gas. Before this trip I contacted the Hudson Bay Company in Winnipeg, requesting so many gallons of aviation gas for each place I stopped. I knew they had caches for their own planes. I planned my whole trip which would take three, four or even five weeks.

Within a few days, I received a telegram from the Hudson Bay people in Winnipeg that said, "You are authorized to draw so many gallons from this cache here, and so many gallons from this cache there and so on -- exactly as I had requested. I was happy about that so off I started. At last I reached one of these places where I was authorized to take quite a lot of their gasoline. I had planned to call at this particular cache twice -- once going north and again going south. A crowd as usual gathered around the plane. Among them I saw the Hudson Bay Manager. He politely waited till I had shaken hands and greeted the Indian folk, including the chief.

Then he came forward and after a brief greeting said, "I hope you don't need any gasoline."

Instead of answering him, I pulled the telegram out of my pocket and gave it to him.

He immediately started to laugh. I asked, "What's the joke?"

He said, "I don't know what's the matter with those people in Winnipeg. They authorize you to take so many gallons of gas from here and we haven't a drop of gas. Come on up to the house and I'll prepare supper. You can stay with us."

Well now, you can imagine my predicament. Here I was out of gas and away up North. What now? At this point the chief came back and asked me, "You want gas?"

I said, "Yes I do need gas but I can't use kicker gas (outboard motor gas), I need airplane gas."

He replied, "Come, I have gas for you." I looked over to the Hudson Bay Manager. He didn't say anything but just shook his head, meaning "No." But one cannot turn an Indian chief off cold, so the least I could do was to follow him.

I spoke to the manager. "You go on up and I'll be over shortly."

The chief led the way and I followed with quite a few people behind us. We reached his abode and went around behind. He stopped, smiled and pointed to a forty-five gallon sealed drum of 80-87 aviation gasoline. I could hardly believe my eyes. He said, "Do you want that?" I replied, "I sure do! Whose is it and where did you get it?" He through the interpreter told me of a man who had flown in with a plane, intending to open up a free

67

fur trading business. He had asked the chief if he would take care of his gasoline. Since then, in fact, just a few months before, this man had crash-landed his plane. The damage was beyond repair and so he wouldn't need the gas.

Well, was I ever glad. Not for the plane accident, but because now I had gas. So I said to the chief, "Do you want me to pay for the gas now, or what do you want me to do?"

He replied, "I don't know. Whatever way you want."

I told him that I had ordered a quantity of aviation gas to come to this place via the tractor train. I also told him that if any pilot is really stuck for gas, you can let him use just enough of mine to get him out, but never take money for it. Always insist that the gas be replaced. Because what is money good for when you need gas? Money is valueless unless you can purchase gas.

"If you wish, I will order an extra forty-five gallon drum to replace this one."

He said that was O.K. so I left a note with the chief stating that I had taken this gasoline and would replace it when the tractor train arrived. The chief was happy and I was more than satisfied.

I made my way over to the Hudson Bay Manager's house. He was frying eggs and had an egg skillet in his hand. As I opened the door, he laughed and said, "Didn't I tell you it was no use?" I replied, "Listen man, I've got a forty-five gallon sealed drum of 80-87 plane gas."

He was so shocked he dropped the skillet on the floor, and said, "If I had known that gas was there, I would have used it a number of times. Several pilots have needed gas but there was none."

But I said, "Well, I guess the Lord saved that gas for me!"

I was able to refuel the plane and deliver my load to the missionary at Fort Severn on Hudson Bay and had enough gasoline left to refuel on my return trip.

During the summer of 1953 we built the church and parsonage at Fort Severn with the help of a few men whom I had flown in. It was the Stone Church in Toronto who provided the finances for this project. The two lady missionaries were still here. One of the men I had flown in was Dan Priest. He knew one of our lady missionaries, Grace Oates for quite some time.

And it was while building here at Fort Severn that they announced their engagement. They were married that fall in Manitoba where Dan came from; then they travelled to Oxford House, Manitoba, where Dan was pastor before coming to Fort Severn. It was on September 9th, 1953, that I flew to Oxford House and took as many supplies as I could handle, and with Grace, now Mrs. Dan Priest, we flew to Fort Severn. Dan wanted his canoe, motor and quite a few things at Fort Severn and had decided to canoe down the Hayes River to Hudson Bay and along the coast to Fort Severn, a distance of approximately four hundred and fifty miles. Dan figured he could make it in about two weeks. In the meantime I flew south to get more supplies and returned to Fort Severn on October 1st. Grace the newlywed was almost hysterical as she told me that her husband Dan had not arrived and she was worried for his safety.

I immediately refuelled the plane, took one of the best Indian guides, and started out looking for Dan. We flew along the Hudson Bay coast, checked on islands and along the rivers which emptied into the Bay. At last we decided to land at Kaskattama River Camp, the only place where we knew some trappers would be living. As we flew over the camp just before dark, we noticed quite a few people outside their log houses. I noticed one man who appeared to be very excited as he waved his arms as we flew over. On landing we found out who this excited man was - it was Dan Priest. He had encountered a lot of trouble on the Hudson Bay and at last left his canoe and supplies and started to walk to Fort Severn. He came across this camp where we found him. You can imagine how glad he was to see us. We spent the night there and the next morning flew back into Ontario to Fort Severn.

We also purchased two buildings in Churchill, Manitoba, that same summer, another project of the Stone Church in Toronto, and moved them to our church lot to form an L shape building for church and parsonage. Rev. and Mrs. George Whittal were our first pastors here. God blessed this work and it wasn't long before the auditorium was filled. Quite a few of them accepted Jesus as Saviour.

I had also been into the Pagwa River Indian Settlement where Mrs. Wraight was teaching school. We often held our services in the school classroom, or in one of the homes. A number of these people committed their lives to Jesus and wanted to have regular services. Mr. and Mrs. Wraight decided to leave Pagwa River after Mr. Wraight built the school building and Mrs. Wraight taught for a number of years. It was on May 8th, 1954 that I received the deed of Mr. and Mrs. Wraight's property at Pagwa River, which they donated to our Northland Mission. We were able to purchase another lot from the Government and a church building was erected, with Pastor Roger Cree in charge. Dedication service was held November 14, 1954.

Also in the month of May, I made a trip to Moosonee to find a lot on which to build a church. It was on May 13, 1954 I went to North Bay to the Ontario Northland Railway offices where I made a deal to purchase a lot in Moosonee for a church building. We began to build here at Moosonee on July 12, 1954 with Arthur Zerbin, Milford Heimbecker and Newell Scarfe helping. Services were held in the public school while we were building the church. Rev. and Mrs. Lawrence Beck were our first pastors here.

My wife and I made a few flights into Wawa, Ontario, beginning July 23, 1952 and had taken Miss Milda Rosenke in to open a church here. She and other lady helpers started a Sunday School in their apartment and later on we were able to organize church services.

As time went on and more native people became born again believers, I realized that in order for the Lord's work to be self-supporting, self-maintained and self-propagated, we must begin to teach and train these Indian people to become pastors and evangelists to their own people. We began to pray that God would place His Hand of blessing on the ones He wanted to choose as leaders. We also began to make plans to open a Bible School to which these students could go and receive this teaching and training.

It was on July 6th, 1955, that we began the Bible School in the mission at Moosonee on the southern end of James Bay. I had been on the lookout for potential students as I visited the settlements in the north. Out of the many who expressed a desire to go to Bible School we chose five for our first class. I had to fly them to Moosonee two at a time.

The furthest flight was a distance of approximately five hundred and fifty miles one way. I brought in groceries beforehand as we had to provide room and board for them. At that time there was no sewage or town water available. So we had outdoor toilets and we carried the water in pails. To supplement our diet, I took some of the students fishing on Saturdays up the Moose River, where we caught pike and pickerel fish.

The Bible School term was for eight weeks and the complete Course covered a three year period. The students were able to participate in the daily devotions as well as in the Sunday and week night services, which gave them practical experience. I flew the first load of students back on September 2nd and returned to Moosonee the next day. The weather closed in and there was no more flying till September 7th.

Flying in the north was a lot of fun, when the weather was nice - but I could hardly make a flight covering five hundred miles without getting into some bad weather. Many times I had to land, put up my tent and wait it out till the weather would clear. Sometimes it was just overnight, sometimes one or two days before I could fly out. So I always had to keep a good survival kit of food, etc. in the plane. At times we got strong wind storms, very turbulent, in fact so rough I wondered how the little plane could hold together. I would have to land on the nearest lake until the winds died down.

It was during these years that radar systems were built across Canada and I was able to fly in and hold services for the construction crews. Many of these flights were made in planes flying freight to these sites such as Canso, DC-3, DC-4, C-46 and other types. I conducted services all across northern Ontario as well as in northern Quebec for their construction men.

In the fall of 1955, I was in southern Ontario conducting missionary meetings in many churches. I also had an appointment with the Department of Transport and had reserved a few days for it. I was able to complete my business with the DOT ahead of schedule and found I had a couple of days to spare. Not wanting to waste any time - as the Bible says to redeem the time - I got on the train from Toronto to Montreal the night of October 27, 1955 and early on the morning of the 28th I was able to get on a C-46 transport plane as a member of the crew and flew up to Great Whale River where a Radar site was being constructed. I conducted a service for the men after which quite a number of them prayed for Jesus to save them. I caught the next plane out for Montreal in time to catch a train to Toronto where I arrived on the morning of October 30 which was a Sunday - in time for my next service.

My motto was, "I am but one, but I am one. I cannot do everything, but I can do something. What I can do, I ought to do, what I ought to do, God helping me, I will do."

It was during the year of 1955 that the Geco Copper Mine was developing their claim at a spot in the wilderness, north and east of Port Arthur and Fort William, and also were building houses for their employees at a town site named Manitouwadge. Three prospectors discovered this copper find and sold out for one million dollars each. It was on January 16, 1956 that Sterling Beaudry and I flew into Manitouwadge to look the place over and start church services. Sterling helped me a great deal in changing over from floats to skis in the fall and vice versa in the spring for many years. The first meeting was held in the school at Manitouwadge on May 24, 1956.

The Indian Bible School at Moosonee started on June 27, 1956 for the second term and my wife Tyyne came up to look after the cooking. She cooked at the Bible School for quite a number of years. It was a full two month course. This term of school closed on August 30, 1956.

I found that the 170 Cessna plane CF-HCO was quite underpowered with the 145 HP engine, especially on floats. There were a number of times during very warm days and no breeze blowing that I could not take off at all. I began to plan on getting a 180 Cessna which would have two hundred and thirty horsepower. I mentioned this to Dan and Grace Priest on August 22, 1956 when I flew them up from South Porcupine to Fort Severn after their return from a holiday in England. Grace immediately gave me five dollars and Dan ten dollars which began our fund for the larger plane.

On October 17th, 1956 my wife Tyyne and Milda Rosenke

and I flew over to a lake just south-west of Hornepayne. Our purpose was to establish a church in this community. We visited around town and arranged for an apartment for Miss Rosenke - also found her employment at one of the local stores. We hurried back to the lake as we wanted to be back home before dark. There was no breeze blowing and I tried to take off three times before succeeding. By the time we got airborne we were getting close to the far shore. It didn't look too good to me and I began to perspire as we just barely missed the trees on our climb out. This was it. I was sure the Lord didn't expect us to fly so dangerously. We needed a more powerful plane for sure.

I mentioned my thoughts about getting a more powerful plane to some of our brethren. One of them said, "John, you have the most costly piece of equipment of all our missionaries. You have a good plane, so be satisfied with what you have!" Well, there wasn't too much encouragement here, but I continued to pray and after awhile I mentioned this matter to another of our men. He asked me what it would cost to trade our 170 Cessna in on a 180 Cessna. I had already checked into this and found that it would cost $10,000.

He then said, "John, we just haven't got that kind of money."

"I'm not asking you for money, not for one red cent," I replied.

"Well," he said, "what are you asking for?"

I replied, "Just the green light to go ahead."

He said, "Do you have faith to trust God for $10,000?"

"Yes," I replied, "I've already prayed about this and I know this is the will of God and that God will provide."

I referred to Psalm 78. The children of Israel murmured against God and complained even after God had done mighty miracles for them. They said in verse 19, "Can God furnish a table in the wilderness?" Yes, they questioned the ability of God and He was angry with them because as verse 41 says, they "limited the Holy One of Israel." God spoke to my heart as I prayed about that $10,000. and the question was whether or not God could provide that $10,000. Were we going to limit God? The answer must be a clear cut "no" or "yes". Well there was only one answer; surely He would provide.

So my good friend said, "Well, if you can believe God for $10,000. you go right ahead." Immediately I put my order in for the plane. That was in the fall of 1956 and I felt by float time in the spring I would want to deal CF-HCO in on the 180 Cessna.

That fall and also in the spring of 1957 I conducted missionary services in our churches across the country and in the United States and I mentioned the need for this better plane. When the date arrived I had the $10,000. as I had promised the fall before. I made the deal and got our first 180 Cessna CF-JAY on April 24, 1957. Praise God for supplying that need.

Throughout February and March of 1957 I flew to many of the Radar sites in the north and conducted services for the construction men. There would be anywhere from thirty to one hundred men in attendance. The Holy Spirit worked in these men's hearts and at the conclusion of each meeting I gave an invitation to any who wanted to come forward and accept Jesus Christ as Saviour. Sometimes there would be three or four come forward for prayer, other times there would be twelve to fifteen who desired to be "born again". I was so thrilled to see the open and honest response to the claims of Christ.

TRANSPORTATION

IN THE NORTH

Indian Dog team.

A twin Otter from Austin Airways used to supply northern Eskimo settlements.

A tractor train which brings supplies to inland settlements once a year during winter months.

The ship comes in once a year at Fort Severn, Ontario's most northerly settlement.

A team of oxen.

CHAPTER 8

PEOPLE AND PLACES

**"And (He) went about . . .teaching . . .and preaching
the Gospel." Matt. 9: 35**

It is such a thrill to be in a service where there are twenty or thirty wonderful Christians, such as at Sachigo. You should hear those precious people praise and worship the Lord, after they are saved. It's just wonderful. They appreciate so much what the Lord has done for them. Different ones would testify and the interpreter would tell me what they said. On many occasions they explained to their own people during a service, that they had always considered themselves Christians. In fact, they had always been taught that they were children of God, till these people came and showed them that all are sinners until they accept Jesus as Saviour.

Often they said, "We have accepted Christ and now we know we are going to Heaven. We don't have to read our prayers any more from a book. We can pray from our hearts." And oh the joyful smiles that radiated from their faces as they told their fellow men of their new found experience.

I remember one service like this. A young girl testified. I think she was about eighteen or nineteen years old. After she witnessed to the saving grace of the Lord Jesus Christ, she closed with a request for prayer. She said, "Will you please pray for my father? He is so sick."

Then she sat down. So I asked her where her father was and what sickness he had.

She replied, "He's been in Brandon Hospital for such a long time and he's getting worse. He has T.B. and we got a letter saying that he is very bad." Tears flowed down her cheeks as she told us this.

I replied, "Our God is able to heal your father and bring him home again. Let's all pray right now and believe God to heal him."

And oh what a prayer meeting we had as we all with one accord cried to the Lord to heal this man.

After service I told them, "You keep on praying and believing and even after I leave tomorrow morning, I'll keep on praying for him too."

It was a few months later in a different part of the North that I landed where there is a small government nursing station at Big Trout Lake. The man in charge came over to the plane and asked where I was going from here and was I alone. I told him where I had planned to fly to, and asked him if he wanted to come along.

"No," he said, "I don't want to go as I have to look after the nursing station. But if you have room, I would appreciate it if you would take a passenger." I said I would be glad to. So after service when I was ready to go I noticed the passenger boarded the plane. He couldn't speak English, so we didn't communicate at all.

From Big Trout Lake, we flew into Bearskin Lake Village where we had a good Gospel service. Afterwards my Indian passenger was back at the plane to continue on with me to Sachigo. By this time evening had set in and a large crowd gathered for another Gospel service.

A number of believers testified of God's hand on their lives, amongst them the young girl who told how wonderfully God answered prayer and healed her father. She was so happy that tears ran down her face as she spoke. I immediately recognized her as the one who requested prayer for her father a number of months before.

As soon as she sat down, I questioned her about her father . . . . "Did you get a letter from him saying that he was healed?"

She said "No, he's sitting over there in the service, he arrived today and you brought him in yourself."

What a time of rejoicing and thanksgiving we had then!

I had flown into the seaplane base here at Nakina and visited quite a number of homes. Several people were interested in opening a Gospel church here; but we needed a worker to move in, get a job, and begin regular services. We prayed about this and visited at the Eastern Pentecostal Bible College in Peterboro, Ontario mentioning the need of a worker. The Lord called Archie Peever to be the young man to accept this challenge and he moved to Nakina in the summer of 1960. It was on September 10, 1960 that I made another flight to Nakina. Archie met the town barber, Alex Darechuk, who was very interested in helping us. Together we looked around for a suitable property for the church. A very good sized lot was purchased from the Anglican church.

June 10th, 1961, we purchased a large building from the Canadian National Railway Co. It was a well built, heavy plank building. We decided that two thirds of this building would be plenty big enough for an auditorium and also for living quarters and Alex Darechuk needed the other one third. We got two chain saws and sawed the one third off the building. We were hoping to be able to move the two thirds part of the building across the tracks and onto our lot. We hired a truck and a large float after jacking the building up.

We moved the float underneath and let the building down. But the building was so heavy the float began to collapse and the truck broke an axle. We eventually had to saw the building in three pieces. It took a number of days to get the repairs made, after which we hired a tractor to help the truck pull the heavy loads, making three trips. At last the two parts were in place on our lot and we were able to join them together. It took a lot of time and work to complete this project but on March 25, 1962 we held the Dedication Service for the Church at Nakina.

The Lord blessed this work, especially among the young people. This group was called Crusaders and boys and girls of this church were excited about the program and wouldn't want to miss it for anything.

It was while here at Nakina that Archie Peever made a trip south. This was a very important trip as he brought back his bride Kathy. Together they did a fine job for the Kingdom of God.

We needed living accommodations for the pastor at Manitouwadge. We were not in a financial position to build a home so we agreed to purchase a trailer to be a temporary home. It was December 28th, 1956 while I conducted a meeting in Windsor, Ontario, that I purchased a trailer from a friend of mine, Mr. Mills. I hauled it north to my home in South Porcupine where it stayed till March 10th, 1957 when Arne Lindholm and I left home pulling this trailer to Manitouwadge. We had quite a trip as Highway 17 was just being built between Port Arthur and Sault Ste. Marie with a branch road into Manitouwadge. Our route was from South Porcupine, Hearst, Geraldton, Nipigon, then eastward to Marathon and northeast to Manitouwadge.

We left home early on the morning of March 10th and were able to make good time on that first day driving fifty to sixty miles per hour. It was quite late that same evening that we pulled into a gas station at Beardmore. Just as we stopped at the gas pump the left wheel on the trailer fell off. Thank God it happened then and not when we were travelling sixty miles per hour. I discovered the axle spindle had broke. It could have been the extreme cold weather which caused it.

Arne and I worked on the trailer far into the night. We made many long distance phone calls to order another axle but could not find one in stock. We removed the old axle and took it up to one of the gold mine welding shops, where they were able to weld it. Now we needed to replace the wheel bearing which was all broken. So we drove approximately one hundred and fifty miles to Port Arthur and got a new wheel bearing. We got everything put back together and started out for Manitouwadge via Nipigon. There was a very steep hill just after we passed Nipigon on the north shore of Lake Superior. I tried to get up speed to carry us over but when we were about three quarters of the way the car wheels began to spin and we came to a stop. Arne jumped out and put a block of wood behind the trailer wheel.

It was nearly midnight so what should we do? I began to make us a bite to eat on the propane stove when I heard a truck coming. Jumping out of the trailer I hailed the truck. The driver was very kind and realized it was dangerous to leave a car and trailer on the hill especially in the darkness of night. He had a good chain handy which he hooked onto us and then he was able to pull us to the top of the hill. The snow plough made a wide spot in the road so we parked off the road overnight. The next day we had very little difficulty in travelling the rest of the way to Manitouwadge.

We hired a bulldozer to push the deep snow back off the lot and we set the trailer in place. Rev. and Mrs. Art Hambleton arrived on March 14th and were able to move into the trailer. They conducted services in the Recreation Hall.

On May 13, 1958 I checked all over Manitouwadge for a lot to build a parsonage church on. Rev. Art Hambleton had accepted the pastorate here and Rev. Clarence Aide held a series of good services in a tent.

It was on July 23, 1958 that I paid $1,155.00 for the building lot. That same day we staked out the size of the building we purposed to build. July 24, we built a small building to keep tools and supplies in and ordered lumber. Men arrived from Port Arthur - Mr. Nyyssonen, and Peterboro - Frank Cunningham and Norman Hubbard. The shovel arrived and dug the basement on July 26. Art Hambleton, the pastor worked at the Geco Copper Mine on the regular day shift and helped us work on the building in the evenings. We poured the footings on August 1st.

I had to fly back to South Porcupine where Rev. Clarence Aide was waiting for me and we flew up to Churchill, Manitoba where Rev. Ken and Mabel Roney were pastoring.

After holding services at a number of settlements enroute, I arrived back at Manitouwadge on August 13 to work on the building. The Geo. Wagner family of Windsor arrived on August 14th to help us build. My wife, Sister Wagner, Sister Hambleton and our boys helped carry the twelve inch cement blocks while the men built up the block walls. The women also cooked the meals for all working on this project.

On October 16 we shingled the roof while electricians worked on wiring the building and the plumbers were busy installing the plumbing. Mr. Grierson and Mr. Jeppel arrived from Ottawa to help us on October 16th.

A Finnish man from Sudbury, Penti Laari also came to help build and in January 1959 he worked on putting the trim on the windows and doors. It was very cold, forty-five to forty-eight degrees below zero F. On January 5th, two men came from Kohls of Pembroke to begin work on installing the oil furnace. Work proceeded slowly through the winter months. The Hambleton's had already moved in. Then on May 25th, 1959 Carson and Norman Hoy and Roy McKnight arrived at South Porcupine from Goderich and we flew over to Manitouwadge to crack fill, paint inside and finish off the outside. While I was in southern Ontario holding services I made a deal on some folding chairs at the factory at Ingersol. These arrived at Manitouwadge on May 29th.

The dedication service was held on July 26th, 1959 when Brother Holbrook started special meetings here. Ken and Mabel Roney who pastored at Churchill, Manitoba arrived at South Porcupine and we flew over to Manitouwadge for the Dedication Service.

I conducted services at Sachigo, Ontario, a small Indian settlement near the Manitoba border in northwestern Ontario, for a few years. These services were held in different homes and we thank the Lord for the number of people who accepted Jesus as Saviour. They mentioned to me a number of times about building a church in which the services could be held. So we made plans to build.

I made an appeal in southern Ontario for men to come and help us. Merle Mintz of Toronto and his nephew Carl Mintz of Brampton responded to this call and they arranged to spend their holidays at Sachigo. They were both willing workers but the only hitch in the plan was that they had to fly in. Merle Mintz especially balked at that idea. He just did not want to get into the plane. But we had no choice as there were no roads into Sachigo. I well remember on June 15, 1957 the three of us climbed into the 180 Cessna JAY after we had loaded a lot of supplies in to take with us.

Carl sat in the back and Merle took the right front seat. Before take off, Merle buried his face away down between his knees. He just didn't like the idea of being up in the air at all. After I had climbed up to 3000' I told Merle what a beautiful day it was and all the nice scenery he was missing, but he was not at all interested. After we had flown for about one and a quarter hours he gradually took a peek out - until his nerves settled and after that he really enjoyed flying.

At Sachigo a number of Indian men went into the spruce bush with us where we cut suitable trees. After we chopped off the limbs and sawed the trees into the right lengths we then had to peel off the bark. One of us would then tie a rope on the end of the log while two or three dug in their cant hooks and we dragged the logs out of the bush and down into the water. After a full day of hard work we made a boom of these logs and hauled them across the lake to our building site with three canoes powered by outboard motors. It was a happy day on September 3rd, 1957 when we held the Dedication Service for the new church.

During the years of flying in the Northland, I would leave word at home as to the approximate time of my return. On one occasion we had some bad storms, very strong winds and blowing snow. I knew I could never make it back home at the time appointed. Our children were quite small and they were getting anxious and excited as day after day they listened for the sound of the plane. One evening the storm was exceptionally bad - blowing trees down and shingles off the houses. My wife told the children that it was too stormy for me to come home. That evening in family devotions they each prayed for my safe return and David, who must have been only about three years old, cried out, "Our Big Jesus can bring my Daddy home!" And Jesus answered their prayers.

I am sure that over the many years it was the cry of their little hearts which the Lord heard and answered.

WORKS FOR THE LORD

Rev. Tom Johnstone visiting the Indian Congregation at Sachigo Lake, Ont.

Our Pentecostal Church in Moosonee, Ontario with Bible School students and teachers.

Building a church on the solid rock at Baie Comeau, Quebec.

CHAPTER 9

BIBLE SCHOOL
"Study to show thyself approved." II Tim. 2: 15

We've had quite a number of men and women come to help us in the Bible School at Moosonee, Ontario which commenced in 1955 with a two month course. To graduate, students must come for the three years term.

Our first missionaries at Moosonee were Rev. and Mrs. Lawrence Beck who arrived October 23, 1954 and assisted in the Bible School the following year.

Others who came to help in the following years were Rev. R. Schwindt, Miss Elsie Chamberlin, Rev. K. Roney, Miss Milda Rosenke, Mrs. Yorth, Mrs. Elizabeth Fraser, Ruth Phillips, Mary Caskey, Tyyne Spillenaar, Eli Chaiarelli, Pauline Bauman, Grace Spillenaar, Ruth Barnewall, Rev. and Mrs. George Whittal, Rev. and Mrs, L. Kubryn, Rev. and Mrs. Harold Howarth, Rev. Robert Price, Rev. M. Case, Rev. and Mrs. Glen Adams, Rev. and Mrs. D. Moulden, Rev. and Mrs. Brian Steed. Brian started with us in 1962 and piloted the missionary plane for a few years. On June 11, 1962 Rev. Ernie Dawe of Doon, Ontario, and Brian Steed and I flew to Moosonee to build the "Fraser House" named after Mrs. Elizabeth Fraser of Ottawa who donated most of the funds for this project. Pastor Don McEwen of Moosonee worked along with us from early morning till late every night. The Dedication of this Fraser House was conducted on August 19, 1962. Other teachers and cooks were Robert Hunter, Rachel Eytcheson, Paul Hacker, Rev. and Mrs. D. McEwen, Ethel Fisher, Larry Bristo, John Knapp, Lillian Geddes.

In 1969 we held our first Bible School at Nakina. We purchased the property in 1968 and after the '68 Bible School at Moosonee we packed up and moved everything over to

Nakina. Pastor and Mrs. Ed Morrison of the Nakina Church were able to help, also Jonathan Chapman. Then in 1970 Paul Johnston and Rev. Dan Tomen came to help teach and Eileen Bennett helped with the cooking. In 1971 Rev. and Mrs. Wm. Moore accepted the pastorate at Nakina and assisted at the Bible School with Mr. Dale Cummins and Mr. and Mrs. Victor Cooper. We must make mention of Robert Boose who was our official photographer to take the pictures needed to publish our Bible School Year Books.

In 1972 Mr. and Mrs. Lloyd Anderson and Vivian Laukkanen taught the classes with my wife Tyyne cooking.

In 1973 Dale Cummins was the principal with Roger and Sharon Larrison helping to teach and Mrs. Rogers and my wife cooking.

We were not entirely satisfied with our Bible School program and after much prayer and consultation decided to sell the Nakina property. Instead of flying the students out we decided to fly the teachers in to spend two weeks in one settlement, then move to another settlement for two weeks, then to the third settlement. With two teams on the go we could reach six settlements each year.

1974 our teacher team was Wayne Greulich and Ivan Robinson who started at Sandy Lake with a good enrollment, the Sachigo Lake and Weagamow. The second team was Paavo Korpela and Paul Johnson who started at Moose Factory. Then we flew them to Big Trout Lake and then to Fort Severn.

Since I have resigned from the Northland Mission work as of January 1976, Mr. Dale Cummins has been appointed as the new Director.

CHAPTER 10

NORTHLAND MISSION POST
"....My God shall supply...." Phil.4: 19

I have referred to Mrs. Elizabeth Fraser of Ottawa who has constantly taken a keen interest in this missionary work. She was full of ideas which she was willing to help put into practice. She often sponsored projects and fully supported them financially. One of these ideas was to open a Northland Mission Post in either South Porcupine or Timmins to handle used clothing, furniture, etc., whatever our northern missions needed.

Actually when Mrs. Fraser first mentioned the idea I didn't want any part of it. We had plenty to do now let alone get involved with this. But Mrs. Fraser was persistent. She said, "Let's try it, and I will pay all expenses. If it doesn't work out to your satisfaction we'll close it up. More than that I'll stay right here and with other women helping we'll see what can be done."

Well, what else could I do when the situation was presented like that? I had nothing to lose. So right away we looked around for a suitable property and found a place that required considerable alterations. After days of cleaning up, building shelves and bins, the Northland Mission Post opened on November 5, 1962.

This new project proved very valuable as time passed. Churches in the south through their Women's Missionary Councils were able to gather good used clothing and ship it up to us. These were all sorted out and placed in their proper places. Each fall hundreds of boxes were packed, tied up, addressed, and shipped by freight as far as possible by rail to where the tractor trains operated from - then out into the wilderness of the north to our missions in the different settlements.

The missions in the western part of northern Ontario were served by the Johnson Company from Ilford, Manitoba and operated to Red Sucker, Manitoba, Sachigo, Ontario, Weagamow, Ontario and all places between. The tractor train composed of a good size Caterpillar bulldozer with a plough on front. This one would break the trail. The next bulldozer hauled a couple of sleighs loaded with bulldozer fuel and had a sleeping caboose and kitchen behind. The third tractor would have four or five sleighs loaded with freight and then another - forming a long train which travelled night and day across the wilderness, lakes, and rivers, weeks on end, to deliver the goods. Later on Sigfusson Co. operated a train for this area from Riverton, Manitoba. Then for the center and eastern part of northern Ontario another tractor train base was set up near Pickle Lake, Ontario to cover all the rest of the north. We shipped tons of used clothing to the different missions each year and the Northland Mission Post proved to be an "arm of the vision" to fill a great need. Then in the spring of the year we again packed tons of clothing in boxes, tied them up well and addressed them to settlements on James Bay and Hudson Bay. At first we had to ship by railway to Churchill, Manitoba where the Hudson Bay Co. boat operated to serve along the coast of Hudson Bay and then to reach settlements in James Bay we shipped to Moosonee where the Hudson Bay Co. had another boat operating in James Bay. This proved to be a great asset to the mission work and met a need among the people of the north. After Mrs. Fraser got things operating in the Northland Mission Post she returned to Ottawa and my wife Tyyne had a job on her hands. Each morning she drove to the store in Timmins, worked hard all day and returned home each night. It was getting to be too much for her so on March 10th, 1963 Mrs. Rachael Etchyson of British Columbia arrived to help us. When she left B.C. the flowers were blooming and the lawn grass was green. Here it was thirty-two degrees below zero F.

The Timmins store proved to be a real help to the Mission work not only for a distribution center but also to meet the needs of families in this area.

The ladies would put a small price on each article and by the end of the year we found that the Northland Mission Post had contributed over $1,000.00 to the mission work after all expenses were paid. Since Rachael Etchyson could handle the Timmins store my wife decided we ought to open one in South Porcupine so on May 22, 1963 we opened a store on Crawford St. in South Porcupine. Both of the stores proved to be a real blessing to the missionary work of the North. God bless Elizabeth Fraser.

CHAPTER 11

BAIE COMEAU, QUEBEC
**"Go ye into all the world and preach the Gospel
to every creature." Mk. 16: 15**

I was greatly concerned about getting the Gospel to some of the larger centres in northern Quebec such as Baie Comeau, Seven Islands, and Schefferville.

I wanted to make a survey visit to these places and mentioned this proposed trip to a few of the pastors when I held missionary services in their churches.

Rev. Ross Schwindt, Vineland pastor, mentioned that he would like to go with me. So on February 11th, 1958 Ross arrived in South Porcupine. We immediately loaded the plane as the weather was perfect for our flight. I filed a flight plan at the Timmins Airport by phone to fly to Roberval, Quebec, where we would have to refuel. After taking off from Porcupine Lake we climbed up to 9000' where we found a strong tail wind. It was a beautiful cloudless day and Ross and I were really enjoying the flight.

All of a sudden Ross dug his elbow into my ribs and I looked over to see what was the matter. There right close to us was a fighter air force jet. It looked like a CF-100. The pilot had lowered his wheels and flaps to slow him down but still he was gaining on us. As soon as he was ahead of us he made a slow right hand turn. I said, "Ross get your camera. He's coming back again." Sure enough, the jet came up slowly beside us again and looked us over. Ross took his picture and by this time he was getting ahead of us again. Apparently he was satisfied and off he flew in an easterly direction. After we landed at Roberval I went into the office to close my flight plan. the operator said, "I've already closed your plan but I had a hard job persuading them that you were here already." In fact we were way ahead of our scheduled arrival time because of the strong tail wind.

We encountered very strong winds and storms on this trip but on February 15th we landed at Schefferville which was then known as Knob Lake. The town was fair size, located just north of Labrador on the Quebec side. There was a radar base here and a good airstrip. After visiting here to see the need of the Gospel we decided to leave on the 17th. The weather turned somewhat milder and a freezing rain fell the night before. All the planes at the airstrip were covered with a good quarter inch of ice. What a mess that was. I inquired about the possibility of a heated hangar to get the plane inside to melt the ice off. I was told the only heated one was the R.C.A.F. hangar and that was strictly for their own planes. I really began to pray, that somehow we might be able to get our missionary plane inside.

I found out the Commanding Officer was a Major Hopkins and I phoned and made an appointment to see him. He was very nice and asked me all about our missionary work all across the northland and why we were here at Knob Lake. I answered all his questions and had an opportunity to witness to him about the Lord Jesus Christ. At last he said, "So you would like to put your plane in our heated hangar."

I said, "Yes, that's why I've come to see you."

"Well," he said, "this is something we never do, but perhaps we can make an exception in this case. Do you want to start your plane up and taxi over or do you want me to send a tractor over to pull it in?"

I said, "Oh, I can get it started and I'll taxi over."

"Never mind," he said. "I'll send a tractor over and we'll put it inside and you just leave it there till this weather clears up and you are ready to leave."

Well - Praise the Lord! You can imagine our great appreciation and delight in knowing our missionary plane, "Wings of the Gospel", CF-JAY, was safe inside the heated hangar, because the weather did not clear up till February 20th at which time we were able to fly out.

On July 6th, 1958 I was back at Baie Comeau, Quebec and met Sister Marion Johnson and also Sister Cameron who were anxious that we commence Gospel services here. Rev. Geo.

Whittal was contacted about coming to Baie Comeau and on September 8th, 1958 Rev. Whittal and I flew in from South Porcupine to look the place over.

Actually we needed the Whittals at Moosonee where they had moved early in 1959. So it was on July 28, 1959 that Rev. and Mrs. Ken Roney and I flew to Baie Comeau, on to Seven Islands and north to Knob Lake (Schefferville). On completing our visit here we flew westward toward the Hudson Bay on July 31st intending to arrive at Great Whale River to refuel. A bad storm caused us to detour southward and we found ourselves approximately seventy miles off course. We decided to land and make camp.

We set up the tent and got a fire going and prepared a meal. The mosquitoes and blackflies were so bad I doubt whether anyone slept very much that night. By five fifteen p.m. the next day the weather cleared up sufficiently for us to fly out. Since we were approximately seventy miles south of our course to Great Whale River on the Hudson Bay I decided we would fly to Fort George on James Bay where we could refuel.

After refuelling we still had enough daylight left to fly on to Moosonee. At that time Mrs. Elizabeth Fraser of Ottawa came up to help my wife cook at the Bible School. Mrs. Fraser took a great interest in the Lord's work. We arrived home at South Porcupine August 2nd and the Roney's left for Battersea, Ontario where they were pastoring.

I anchored CF-JAY the 180 Cessna plane, Wings of the Gospel, offshore so that children would not tamper with it. Then we had to make a car trip to Toronto and Orillia and returned home August 7th.

Much work had piled up in my office, and during the next week I worked from early morning to late at night to get caught up. On August 12th while working in my office I heard the wind begin to blow quite strongly. I thought I ought to go to the lake and check the plane. About halfway down the stairs, the phone rang. I hastened to answer it.

The man said, "Come quick your plane has broken loose and is in danger of capsizing." I hurried to the lake to find that two men had already tried to rescue the plane, but as we watched, the plane turned over and sank beneath the waves. That was a great blow to us. I phoned the insurance company in Toronto and they sent Jack Dawson up the next day as he was the insurance adjustor.

Jack Sanderson, the man from whom we had purchased the plane, also came up to assist in recovering the plane. We worked the rest of that day and through the night till one a.m. before we got it to shore and right side up. We then removed the wings, loaded it in a transport truck and shipped it to Toronto.

This was a busy time of year and we could ill afford to be without a plane. I was told it would take a number of months to have JAY flying again. Jack Sanderson of Sanderson Aircraft Co., where we purchased JAY, leased me another 180 Cessna to use in the meantime. On August 24 I flew it from Toronto to South Porcupine. Then on August 25 to Moosonee in time for the closing of the Bible School and headed west with the first load of students. After a flying ministry in the north I returned this plane to Toronto and on September 14th made a deal to purchase our second 180 Cessna CF-LGT (Let God Through), a 1959 model.

All the services at Baie Comeau so far were held in homes. But we planned to build a church as soon as possible. Since Baie Comeau was a company town we had to deal with the company town planning board. I had looked around town at several suitable church sites but when I approached the chairman of the planning board he always found some excuse why he could not permit us to build.

This happened several times over a few months period and at last I got exasperated. I asked him the reason why he always turned us down.

"Well," he said, "if you really want to know, we do not want you people to build a church here in Baie Comeau, and I will do everything in my power to keep you out."

Oh, oh, so that's what it was all about. We will have to work from a different angle. I told the chairman, that the Christians at Baie Comeau had been praying for a church to be built and that's what we planned to do. The head office of the Baie Comeau Paper Mill was at Thorold, Ontario.

On August 3, 1960 I phoned the head office in Thorold to have a talk with the president. I was informed that the president was sick and unable to see anyone. I then asked for the vice president who was Mr. Sewell. I asked him for an appointment. He said that was impossible, as I was away up north at South Porcupine and he in Thorold and he would be leaving for New York the next day at noon. I told him that I could plan to be in his office by ten o'clock next morning if he would see me. He agreed.

That same evening, August 3rd, my son David and I flew from South Porcupine to Port Dalhousie near St. Catharines. I circled, looking for a place to land and decided on a wide creek flowing into Lake Ontario. Next morning we walked into Mr. Sewell's office exactly at ten a.m. Was he ever surprised to see us.

He asked how we made it all that distance. We explained to him that we had flown down the night before in our missionary plane and that the situation at Baie Comeau was so urgent we just had to come.

Mr. Sewell was a very gracious man. He asked all kinds of questions and I answered them as frankly as I possibly could. At last I had to tell him what the Chairman at Baie Comeau had told me.

Immediately I saw a change come over his face. He appeared to be quite indignant at what had happened. He picked up the phone and called the Baie Comeau office. He talked in French and I could not understand exactly what was said but I could tell from the tone of his voice that he was "laying down the law".

After the phone call Mr. Sewell said, "You go back to Baie Comeau and you will be able to purchase three lots for a church, parsonage, and also a parking lot. On August 18, 1960 Rev. Tom Johnstone and I flew to Baie Comeau to pick out a site on which to build the church.

It was February 27th, 1961 on my return from Labrador and Newfoundland that I stopped in at Baie Comeau and Rev. Roney who now pastors here, and I checked the purchase of the church lots. There was a lot of rock in this area and we made a contract with an excavating company to remove sufficient rock at a cost of $9,000.00. This was left in abeyance for the time being. Then on July 19, 1961 while flying through to Seven Islands, Rev. Roney and I decided on a site at 309 Babel St. where the engineers estimated it would cost $1,300.00 to remove the rock for a basement. In the meantime Rev. and Mrs. Carl Verhulst accepted the pastorate here.

On November 17, 1961 Albert Kopare, Floyd Harman and I drove in my car from South Porcupine to Baie Comeau to work on the new church building. Mr. Wm. Reid and Arnold Bell of Oshawa had the architectural plans made up. Both of these men arrived with a three quarter ton truck loaded with windows on November 22, 1961 for this new building. The excavating company men were still removing rock for the basement so on November 24th, Floyd Harman and I made a car trip to Seven Islands to visit the workers there, Miss Erna Klein and Miss Shirley Wicks. We appreciated these ladies who were willing to come and get jobs, maintain an apartment and conduct Gospel services.

My next visit to Baie Comeau was on January 31, 1962 when Mr. Chris Anderson, the Finnish Pastor, Rev. Itkonen and I flew from South Porcupine to work on the church building. We were able to get a lot of work done in a short time. It was on May 27, 1962 that Brian Steed and I flew to Pembroke, landed in the Ottawa River, and met with Basil Cotnam who had a furnace and sheet metal business. The three of us flew to Quebec City where we refuelled and then flew through to Baie Comeau to install the furnace and duct work which Basil had sent in from Pembroke a couple of weeks before. We worked from early morning till late at night as usual and on May 31 we completed the job in time to fly back to Pembroke, Ontario before dark. There was still much work to be done on the inside of the building which took all summer to complete. The Dedication Service was held on January 20, 1963 with Rev. G. Greenwood, Superintendent of Eastern Ontario and Quebec District as speaker.

This work has progressed very nicely and quite a number of people, both French and English have found Jesus Christ as Saviour here.

CHAPTER 12

LABRADOR AND NEWFOUNDLAND
"....unto the uttermost part of the earth." Acts 1: 8B

During my travels I met some of the men of the Newfoundland Assemblies who were interested in me visiting their missions in Labrador and the northern part of Newfoundland. It was arranged that Rev. Albert Vaters meet me in Goose Bay, Labrador and accompany me.

On February 3rd, 1961 I loaded Wings of the Gospel, CF-LGT, refuelled and started on my flight alone from South Porcupine. The weather was fine but it was thirty-two degrees below zero F. I had a good flight, non stop to Roberval where I landed and refuelled - then off again for Baie Comeau. Rev. and Mrs. Ken Roney were there and I spoke at the service that Friday night. The next day was fair weather but Rev. Roney wanted me to stay over to see what we could do about getting the church building lots settled. Our church lot business was limited because of it being Saturday, so we decided that I stay for the Sunday services. It was nice to see quite a few new faces in the service enjoying the presence of the Lord. On Monday we made definite progress in obtaining a suitable site. Tuesday, February 7, I preheated the plane, got my maps in order, and flew to Seven Islands, refuelled, then off again across country to Goose Bay, Labrador, a distance of approximately three hundred and fifty miles.

Pastor Newman who had a church here and Albert Vaters who flew in from St. John's Newfoundland met me at the Military Airport. We had a good service at Rev. Newman's church that night with a large crowd in attendance. The next day we purchased supplies and got all our maps and things ready for our trip. Another service was held at the church. The following day was not too good for flying as the weather had closed in. Rev. Newman and Albert Vaters asked me if I was sure I could find the little settlements which we were to visit. I said if they were on the map I believed I should be able to find them. The first place they wanted to visit was Postville so we checked the map to find it. But it wasn't there. One of the local men said, I know exactly where it is and I can mark it on your map, which he did. I was hoping his mark was on the right spot. I was asked how long it would take to fly from Goose to Postville so I figured it out and gave them my answer.

On February 10th we took off. This was the roughest country I had ever flown and I prayed for the Lord to help me navigate. Our time was just about up. Albert and Rev. Newman were getting perturbed and wondered if we were lost. We had about two more minutes to go as far as my allotted time for the flight was concerned, but no sign of any village at all. High mountains and very deep valleys were all around. Then as I looked over the side of the plane down into a narrow canyon I noticed some buildings. "That's it!" Pastor Newman said. So I circled around and descended down between the canyon walls and landed on the river below. Was I ever glad to know that this was indeed the place we were supposed to arrive at. The people here were happy to see us and it was just thrilling to have a part in their service.

In many churches the services would be of one hour length, but here in Labrador the services often lasted for three and four hours and still the people were not in a hurry to leave. When the Holy Spirit is moving upon hearts and God's power is in action, time goes so quickly. We spent Sunday here. The temperature was thirty-three below zero.

Our next flight was to Cartright and we had a good time here and again the people were delighted to see someone from the "Outside". The pastors here were Rev. and Mrs. Gibb Davidson. Mrs. Davidson - Ruth, was one of our first missionaries up at Ford Severn, Ontario on the Hudson Bay. After leaving there, she and Brother Davidson were married and had come to Cartright to pastor. It was nice to see Ruth again.

My plane radio was beginning to give us trouble and I decided it should be fixed. On February 14 we returned to Goose Bay where we had it serviced. The next day we flew to Carol Lake where the Wabush Mine was located. A church had already been started here at the townsite called Labrador City, with services held in homes. It was on February 17th that we flew over the Grand Falls, as it was then called, but later changed to Churchill Falls. This falls is much higher than Niagara Falls. We landed back at Goose Bay to refuel and overnight, then on the 18th to Charletown where another church was being pioneered by Rev. Gillete. I've always called this place a "one horse town" because true enough there was only one horse in the town. The people here as well as other settlements along the Labrador Coast made their living chiefly by fishing. Port Hope Simpson was our next stop and I'll never forget the services here. The church building was packed full for every service and each service lasted for three or four hours. It is wonderful to see all these people "on fire for God".

It was on February 21st that we flew across the Strait of Bell Isle into Newfoundland. We were able to visit at Grequist, St. Antony, Roddrickton before ending our trip at St. John's. All in all it was a wonderful experience seeing what God was doing in that area of Canada. On February 25th I returned alone to Roddrickton where I refuelled and filed my flight plan to Seven Islands, a distance of over five hundred miles. The flight was uneventfull until I was within one hundred and fifty miles of Seven Islands where I flew into quite a snow storm. I radioed to Seven Islands and was told the weather there was not good at all. I decided to go as far as I could and if necessary I could find a suitable place to land and camp. But I was able to keep going and I reached Seven Islands. The radio operator mentioned that the airport was closed because of the bad weather, but while I circled around I could see a little of one runway. I requested permission to land which was quickly granted, and I was sure glad to be back on terra firma again.

PEOPLE IN THE NORTH

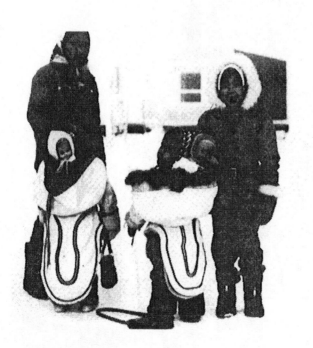

Eskimos.

An Eskimo woman out shopping.

Outside view of an Igloo with a block of ice for a window.

Inside an Eskimo Igloo showing doorway where one must crawl in or out on all fours.

An Eskimo at Ivujivuk, Quebec carving soapstone.

Qolingo playing guitar, Rev. Napartuk and a few Eskimos in a house meeting in Povungnituk, Quebec.

Leonard Thirsk, left of Komoka, Ontario and Karl Kristensen, a school teacher at Ivujivuk, Quebec.

An Eskimo settlement in the summertime.

Elizabeth and Qolingo Tookaluk and Rev. Napartuk, all Eskimos living at Povungnituk, Quebec.

A frozen caribou at an Indian Camp in Northern Ontario.

CHAPTER 13

MIKE ANDERSON'S HEALING
"They shall lay hands on the sick and they shall recover." Mk. 16: 18B

During our ministry in the north, we have seen quite a number of miracles of healing. As the Word says in Mark, "They shall lay hands on the sick, and they shall recover." I'll never forget this one incident of healing which took place on June 24th 1961. I was flying students from the settlements in the north to the Moosonee Bible School. I had a full load of students from Red Sucker, Manitoba and Sachigo, Ontario and we landed at Big Trout Lake to refuel from my gas cache there. A large crowd gathered around, as we were pumping the gas from the barrels into the gas tanks in the plane. One young Indian lady pushed her way through the crowd to where I was and said, "Mike Anderson wants to see you."

I replied, "If Mike Anderson wants to see me, he can come here, because we are in a hurry and after refuelling we want to leave immediately for Moosonee."

"Oh," she said, "he cannot come. He's sick in bed and wants you to go and pray for him."

"Oh, that's different," I replied. "We will come, just as soon as we finish refuelling if you show us the way to his place."

In just a few minutes, the lady led us to Mike Anderson's home - followed by the large crowd. It was a three room building made of logs. The first room was quite large and many of the people were packed inside while the rest waited outside. I found Mike on a board bed in one of the other two rooms. Through the Interpreter I began to talk to Mike about salvation, as I knew that the greatest miracle of all was when one accepts Jesus as Saviour. While I tried to read different portions of scripture and explain them, Mike began to laugh. I wondered, what kind of man is this - just laughing at me, when I was trying to explain to him the way of salvation. So I asked him what he was laughing at. He said, "You have a very short memory. You forgot that I and five other men accepted Jesus as Saviour in your meeting a few months ago."

Well, that settled that question. Then I knew that Mike was a "born again" believer. So now I found and read a few scriptures about healing - that Jesus Christ is the same yesterday, today and forever. Again Mike began to laugh and said, "I know all that. All I want you to do is to pray for me and I know Jesus will heal me."

Well, well, that was real faith. So we prayed for Mike quickly and then we left for Moosonee.

A few months after this I was at Pickle Lake for a service. God blessed in that service and quite a few of the Indian people came forward to accept Jesus as Saviour. Then a few others came to be prayed for for healing. After the service different ones came to shake hands with me including this one woman. She appeared to know me and she laughed as she shook hands. She did act somewhat different than the others, so I asked her name. She said, "Mrs. Anderson." But I could not remember an Anderson at Pickle Lake.

"No," she said, "I'm from Big Trout Lake."

"Oh, are you Mike Anderson's wife?" I asked.

She laughed again as she said, "Yes."

I asked how her husband was, as I had not been to Big Trout Lake since we prayed for him.

"Oh," she said, "he had been sick in bed for many days before you came, but after you prayed and left, he got up and dressed and has been well ever since."

Praise the Lord. He is our Healer as well as our Saviour.

CHAPTER 14

CHURCHILL, MANITOBA

"Ask, and it shall be given you . . . ." Matt. 7: 7

It was on July 15th, 1959 that I flew to Churchill, Manitoba to help Rev. Ken and Mabel Roney pack up and move. Ken Sweigard, his wife Audrey and family arrived on July 17th to take over the pastorate here. A lovely farewell service for the Roney's was held as well as a welcome service for the Sweigard's on Sunday, July 19th.

I'll never forget the incident which happened here on Februay 17, 1962. Rev. Allan Mallory and I had flown to quite a number of settlements in Northern Ontario including Fort Severn which is on the Hudson Bay and is the most northerly settlement in Ontario. We arrived at Fort Severn on February 15th and had very good services for the people here in our church. The next day the temperature was forty-four below zero F. and Rev. Mallory and I attempted to take off for Churchill. The air strip marked off on the Severn River was very rough and our right axle broke. With the help of the Catholic Priest Rev. Morin we jacked the plane up and made temporary repairs so I could fly alone to Churchill for proper repairs including a new axle. The next day was bitterly cold. I did not like the idea of taking off on that rough strip, but what else could I do in that isolated place? It was an easier take off being alone in the plane and I was glad to get air borne. After circling and gaining altitude I began to check to see that everything was working properly. All the instruments appeared normal on the dash. I leaned over to check the left wheel ski combination; it too looked good. Then I reached away over on the right after loosening my seat belt and was able to take a look at the right wheel ski combination. I didn't like what I saw at all. Instead of the ski being level, there it was standing on end, the front of the ski pointing down and the rear of the ski up.

Now what should I do? To return to Fort Severn wouldn't help the situation at all. So I decided to fly through to Churchill, an uneventful flight as the weather was nice. When twenty five or thirty miles out from Churchill I radioed in requesting airport information. I was told to continue on in and call them when I approached the airport. I told the radio operator that I had a damaged right ski and requested permission to fly past the control tower so he could look at it and advise as to landing procedure. My request was granted and I flew past the control tower at an altitude even with the tower for him to check the ski. I waited for him to call me but he didn't call. So I called him asking what he thought of it.

He said, "Make a 180. We want to take another look at it." I turned back and flew past the control tower the second time. Again I waited for his advice but after waiting for quite a while I called him asking for advice.

He said, "You must land sometime so you may as well land now on runway so and so (I've forgotten the particular number of the runway).

By this time I was out over the Hudson Bay. I wondered if I could help my situation. So I radioed back and told him that I would try to straighten out the ski before coming in to land.

He said, "You can try it if you like." So holding onto the steering wheel with my left hand I reached over with my right hand and was able to open that door. I then reached into the baggage compartment and got my shot gun which I had for survival. Holding onto the end of the barrel and putting the butt end through the door I tried to reach down and push the rear end of the ski back and down. But my reach was limited and at last I gave up the idea. I pulled the gun back in and shut the door. As I circled back toward the airport I called the control tower that I was unable to straighten the ski and that I was coming in.

He said, "O.K. we are waiting for you." Then I noticed the big hangar door open and a red truck with flashing lights raced out and down about three quarters of the runway. Then a second red truck with flashing lights came racing out and parked off the runway about half of the way down. Then a third red truck with flashing lights raced down to about a quarter of the way and backed off. "Oh, oh, I thought, is it that bad?"

I really prayed and asked the Lord to help me, somehow. I lined up with the runway. I felt that instead of trying to make a normal landing I should "mush in", hold the nose up as high as possible and keep the tail down as low as possible without creating a stall. By this time I was really perspiring as I again asked the Lord to help and protect me.

Just before contact with the runway with the plane in a "mush" attitude, the lower end of the ski caught the snow covered part of the runway and instead of the plane flipping upside down as was expected, the ski straightened out to level position. Man oh man, was I ever glad to be down safely! I still had my radio open and I could hear the operator breathe a sigh of relief. I requested permission to taxi to a company hangar for repairs. He said, "The whole airport is yours. Taxi wherever you want to. We are just so glad you are safe."

January 25th, 1963 was a sad day for the pastor and congregation at Pagna River. Miss Schultz, the pastor was preparing for service and had taken a lamp into the clothes closet as there was no electricity. The lamp came in contact with a nylon dress which burst into flames. In just a few minutes the whole parsonage was burnt to the ground. Miss Schultz burnt her hands and lost everything she owned. Next day she called me in South Porcupine. My wife and I immediately took the trailer with supplies and drove through to Pagwa. We arranged for her to stay in the Lands and Forest building after getting permission from the Kapuscasing office.

Plans were made to start building a new parsonage in the summer. Money had to be raised in missionary meetings that spring, but in the meantime we must visit the other settlements in the north.

CHAPTER 15

WEATHER PLAYS HAVOC
". . . .He shall give his angels charge over thee." Psa. 91: 11

Before taking off for flights into the north I file a flight notification listing the many settlements I plan to visit. Some of these flights last for one or two weeks or even three weeks. I usually plan on arriving at some place where the Department of Transport had a weather office, where I close my flight notification and if needed, file another.

On February 15, 1963, I started out on such a flight and on February 22 I was at Ilford, Manitoba. The weather was beautiful, not a cloud in the sky, so we were not delayed during the whole week. I radioed Churchill the day before when I was flying from Red Sucker to Ilford to inquire about their weather. They answered 0 0 which meant zero visibility and zero ceiling, in other words, no flying at all. On the 22nd I had planned to fly to Churchill if at all possible.

While warming up my engine on the lake at Ilford I radioed Churchill again and stated that the weather here was CAVU (Ceiling And Visibility Unlimited). Again their answer came back 0 0. So I said that I would fly as far as I could and would keep in touch with them by radio. On and on I flew with perfect weather conditions but as I neared Churchill I could see this huge storm stretched out in front of me as far as I could see to the east and west. But on I flew until I came very near the airport and along side of the storm.

I could see a part of one runway and decided I had enough room to land on wheels if they would give me permission. I radioed in and told them what I had in mind. My request was granted and down I came as slow and low as possible. I touched down and by the time I stopped the plane I was right into this thick storm. I couldn't see a thing. I had to open my left hand door and taxi to the left till I found the white line on the edge of the runway. I followed that, taxiing very slowly until I came to a taxi strip to one of the hangars. Ken Sweigard the pastor was very surprised to see me that day.

Before leaving on one of my northern missionary itineraries I filed a flight notification with the Department of Transport, that I would be visiting quite a number of villages throughout northern Ontario and northern Manitoba, and that I planned to arrive at Churchill, Manitoba at a certain time on a certain day. I always allowed myself at least one extra day a week for bad weather. So on a three week itinerary, I allowed myself an extra three days. But on this particular trip, the weather was excellent as I flew from village to village holding services in each of them. At last, I was flying toward Churchill and found that I was one day early. When I was within approximately twenty five miles of Churchill, I radioed in, giving my location and time of arrival.

Immediately the radio operator called back seemingly quite angrily and said, "What are you doing in this area, at this time. You are not supposed to arrive until tomorrow afternoon."

I replied that I had made better time than I expected and that I would far sooner be a day early than even half an hour late.

"Yes," he said, "but no planes are supposed to be in this area at this time. We are testing 'side winder missiles' and if that last missile fired would have performed properly, you would have been blown to bits."

Apparently these are the missiles used in war, when fired on the ground have a "heat seeker element" built into it, and this guides the missile right to the plane, because of the engine heat.

That was bad news for me, but thanks to God that last missile malfunctioned and was destroyed by remote control.

I apologized to the radio operator and told him that I was unaware of the testing.

He asked, "What are you doing? Where are you going from here?"

My mind was filled with what he had already told me, about being blown to bits, and I thought that's what he meant, if

I was blown to bits, where would I go. So I replied, "I would go to Heaven."

"Oh," he said, "I did not mean that. I mean where are you going from Churchill and when are you planning to leave?"

So you see, once again God had His protecting Hand upon me, and saved me from being "blown to bits".

But to a child of God, sudden death would be sudden glory. It does pay to be ready at all times, as we never know when our time comes.

CHAPTER 16

PAGWA RIVER
" . . . .A time to build . . ." Ecl. 3: 3B

June 12, 1963 Mr. and Mrs. Gordon Selkirk of Ottawa volunteered to help build the new parsonage at Pagwa River. I ordered a railway boxcar load of lumber, insulation, roofing shingles, etc., etc., and we went in on the train from Hearst. There was no siding here at Pagwa River so the whole train was held up for approximately one and a half hours as we unloaded the boxcar, throwing lumber and supplies on both sides of the track.

We needed gravel and sand to make concrete slabs for the posts, so we borrowed a canoe and went up the Pagwa River and to the other side where we found a good supply and carried it up in pails. A Finnish man Mr. Hulko and our son David arrived by train to help us on June 15th. Black flies and mosquitoes were very bad and we used nets around our heads to help keep the flies and mosquitoes out.

We cut the studding and framed in for the doors and windows and raised the walls up one by one. I had to leave by train for Hearst on June 21st where I left my car, to look after purchasing supplies for the Bible School at Moosonee and also to purchase more supplies for Pagwa such as electrical wiring, boxes, etc. I was back on the job by June 26th when we put up the rafters and ceiling joist. We soon were sheeting up the walls and roof and nailing on the shingles. Mrs. Selkirk and Naida Schultz the pastor cooked the meals for all of us as my wife was cooking at Moosonee Bible School. Mr. Hulko and I left on the train on July 7th as I had some business to look after at Hornepayne. Then on July 9th we drove to Fred Rose's farm at Hilliardton and butchered a beef for the Moosonee Bible School which Mr. Rose had donated. I flew the meat and other supplies to Moosonee on July 10th.

More groceries and supplies were needed at Pagwa River which I purchased at Timmins and on July 17, Gus Nelson of South Porcupine and I drove to Hearst with a car load of supplies in time to catch the morning train into Pagwa River. The work was progressing nicely and we installed a metal chimney. On July 25 Mr. and Mrs. Selkirk and I packed up and got the train to Hearst and drove through to South Porcupine where we arrived at three a.m. next morning. My office work had piled up and had to be taken care of.

Basil Cotnam of Pembroke who had installed the oil furnace at Baie Comeau church sent a furnace through to Pagwa River. Mr. and Mrs. Cotnam arrived at our home on August 2nd, 1963 and we left at four a.m. the next morning to drive to Hearst in time to catch the train to Pagwa River. David Spillenaar was still working away on the building and now Miss Schultz had another helper to help cook the meals - Mrs. Cotnam. As usual we worked from very early morning till late at night and completed the duct work and installation of the furnace in time to catch the train at six thirty p.m. August 8th and arrived home at two a.m. next morning.

CHAPTER 17

A QUITTING MYSTERY
"Lo, I am with you alway . . . ." Matt. 28: 20

Mr. and Mrs. Alf Huntley of Florida were waiting for me at South Porcupine as I had asked Alf to go with me on a flight into the north to visit different settlements and hold services. We departed South Porcupine on August 10th to Moosonee where the Bible School was in session. We spent Sunday the 11th here and ministered in the Sunday School and both adult services. On the 12th we flew non stop to Fort Severn where the church was packed full for the service that night. On the 13th we flew to Kasabanica and held a service there in the forenoon. We were requested to fly a very sick baby to the nursing station at Big Trout Lake which we were glad to do. After visiting a few homes here we flew on through to Sachigo where another large crowd was waiting for us at the church.

The next day August 14 we flew on over to Ponask Lake where quite a number of the Sachigo people were fishing. Here we had an outdoor service among the trees. The people sat on the ground and joined in singing so heartily as only believers can do. That evening we flew to Red Sucker, Manitoba for another service. On the 15th we took two more men making four of us and we flew to Island Lake, Manitoba. Here a large crowd gathered of almost two hundred people and we held the service on the shore of the lake in a clearing. Fifteen of the people came forward professing Christ as Saviour and nineteen or twenty came for prayer for healing.

After the service we loaded the plane to return to Red Sucker. It was a normal take off, as we left the lake and began our climb over the trees. But just then the engine faltered and quit. In my training I was always told that if we ever had engine failure on take off never attempt to circle back as it usually resulted in a stall or spin, but always make as good a landing as possible straight ahead, even in the bush. I've had engine failure before but it was later on after take off. But here we were, a full load of passengers and engine failure at the most crucial time.

I called upon the Lord to help us as I swung the plane around and we glided back into the lake. Man, was I ever glad to be safe on the water again.

I got out on the float and checked the engine and drained some gas from the carburetor. Then I started the engine. It sounded good so I taxied around quite a lot and everything appeared normal. Off we flew again, and the second time the engine faltered and quit in about the same place as before. With another prayer for help we swung around and made it back to the lake.

Well, this was really going too far. So I told the other men that I would not try again until I had an engineer check the engine and find out what was the matter. I was informed that there was an engineer down the lake about eighteen miles at the fish processing plant.

I told my men to wait for me here and I would taxi all the way down if necessary. I had restarted the engine again but certainly wasn't going to attempt another take off with a load of people. So I began to taxi, alone, and after a while I decided that since I was over water all the way, perhaps I would try to take off and fly low. The take off was normal, the engine sounded good, and I climbed up a few hundred feet, and in a short time I found the processing plant on an island.

I landed, tied up to the dock, met the engineer and told him what had happened. He checked the plane thoroughly, but could not find anything wrong. He said it must have been a little water or dirt in the gas but it looked as if our troubles were over.

So I flew back and got my passengers back in the plane and this time I took off over the lake and climbed up a few hundred feet before crossing over the shore line. Everything worked well and we flew on over to Red Sucker where we held another service that night.

Next morning, August 16th, we flew over to Ilford,

Manitoba. We then returned to the lake to fly to Churchill. Just after take off as we were climbing up over the bush the engine faltered and quit again. We managed to get back in the lake again. An engineer was working on another plane and we got him to come over to check ours as he had seen what happened. He did quite a thorough check, drained a lot of gasoline out, started the engine up and it sounded good. He said it must have been water or a little dirt in the gas but after checking the gas he could not find any sign of water or dirt. So away we flew to Churchill without further incident.

Ken Sweigard was pastor then and asked if I would fly him and another man out fishing for a couple of hours. I was happy to do so. After refuelling the plane, the three of us took off from Landing Lake and headed north west. We climbed up to about 1200 feet and had just crossed the Churchill River a short distance when without warning the engine quit. I was just talking to the radio operator at the control tower and had filed my flight notification. So I called the operator back and told him our predicament. I said it looks as if we'll have to land in Button Bay, which is part of Hudson Bay. The winds were blowing very strong and I wondered if we would make it. But then, I thought perhaps we can turn around and with a tail wind make it to the Churchill River. I told the operator this, as I swung the plane around. We just made it to the river and landed. What a relief to be safe again. With the strong wind and the strong river current the plane swung around and began going backward down river. The man in the back seat said, "Do you know where we are?"

I said, "Yes, we are in the plane in the Churchill River."

"Yes I know that," he said, and as I turned to see him, he had turned a deathly white. "But we are just above the rapids and the river is full of rocks." Oh, oh, oh, that's not so good, but what can we do? By this time a search and rescue helicopter had flown over from the airport and asked by radio if he could help us.

I said, "Yes, we do need help, but how can you help us?"

He replied he would have to return to the airport as his fuel was very low and that he would return. So away he went. You can be sure that I was praying and asking the Lord to help us as he raced downstream backward. One float touched a rock but it wasn't too hard and I felt that no damage was done. It was so exciting and we were helpless to do anything but ride the plane backward.

The radio operator came back on the air and said that two search and rescue parties were on their way from the airport to the river with boats and would be able to help us. That sounded good to me. But then he added the winds were blowing at thirty-five miles per hour and would increase to fifty miles an hour anytime now. That wasn't good news at all.

By this time we had passed on down through the rapids. I am sure the Lord was directing the plane as we were helpless to steer it at all. Now we were in the big part of the river in the harbour where the ocean going ships came in for grain. With the strong wind the waves were high and the little plane was tossing like an egg shell. It was so rough the search and rescue men could not launch their boat to come out. It looked as if we would be driven on down through the harbour and out into the Hudson Bay. If so, all our hope of being rescued was gone. But the wind changed slightly and blew us over toward the east shore where we landed just short of Hudson Bay. The search and rescue men were waiting for us and one of them said, "Man, you are lucky."

"No," I said, "we are not lucky, but it was the Lord who protected us."

For the next seven days we worked on that plane engine. I got two engineers from Lamb Airways and they worked hard trying to find the trouble. They thought perhaps it would be OK for a test flight after making some adjustments. I test flew the plane six different times and every time it quit, but I made sure I was over the water each time. At last we called the Pan American engineer at the airport and told him the whole story and asked if he could help us.

Even without looking at the plane he said, "After the other engineers had checked everything it's no use for me to look at it. But it looks as if your trouble is definitely in you carburetion. We'll phone to Winnipeg and order another carburetor and it should be here on the morning flight." Sure enough it arrived and he removed the old carburetor and installed the new one.

He said, "OK, test fly it." By this time you can imagine

how I felt after a total of ten engine failures on this one trip and now I am asked to try again. I climbed in, started up, took off, climbed and circled for about fifteen minutes. No more trouble You can imagine our great relief.

After the test flight on August 24th, Alf Huntley and I loaded the plane and headed south. We stopped at quite a few places and held services along the way to Moosonee and South Porcupine, but had no further plane engine trouble.

By August 31st I was back to Pagwa River with more supplies for the new parsonage. While we worked on the building I also conducted the church services on Sundays and usually two or three times during the week. On September 1st we held a water baptismal service in the Pagwa River. The candidates had accepted the Lord as Saviour previously and now wanted to follow Jesus in the waters of baptism. All through the north we hold many water baptismal services every summer and it's a great joy to see these new believers mature and growing in the Lord, obedient to the Word of God. Some of the local Indian Christians helped us work on the building - both men and women, especially Eddie Gillis and Richard Ferris.

Each year in the spring and fall I itinerated in the south conducting missionary meetings and showing my 16mm coloured pictures of the north. The offerings raised were used in the Northland Mission work.

On December 11, 1963 I just arrived home from the south when the phone rang. It was long distance from Hornepayne telling of a fire in the basement of the parsonage church. Quite a lot of smoke damage, but after I went in and inspected the place I figured $1,000.00 would cover the expenses of repair. Our insurance company was willing to pay this amount.

January 11th, 1964 found us back at Pagwa River Parsonage working on the inside of the building. My son Daniel, Brian Steed and I went in by train from Hearst where we left my car. We were able to do much of the electrical work as well as the trim and finishing work such as hanging doors, etc. We got one of the electricians from the Radar Base to inspect and finish off the electric system. More supplies were needed and on February 3rd I flew a load of supplies in by plane.

Bill Lee of Sudbury, Ontario now accepted the pastorate

here as Miss Naìda Schultz had resigned. From Pagwa River I flew to Calstock for a service where Brother and Sister Hubert Bluff were the workers in charge. About sixty people attended the service here. Then on February 5th I flew to Hornepayne for a service and to check on the repairs made after the fire. I arrived at Manitouwadge on the 8th where Rev. and Mrs. Hannaford were pastors and doing a great work. Attendance was good on Sunday the 9th in spite of the forty-two degree below zero weather.

My next stop was at Nakina where Rev. and Mrs. Archie Peever were pastors. Again a good crowd was in attendance and usually in all these services there would be one to four people come for prayer for salvation. On Feburary 11th I flew to Pickle Lake for another service and drove out to Dog Hole where twelve came forward to accept Jesus. On the 13th I flew to Miminska and held a Gospel service with good attendance in the forenoon and ten made decisions for Christ. Then in the afternoon I flew on through to Fort Hope for another wonderful service that night. So on and on we flew, day after day after day, stopping in each place for one service or sometimes two or three but always finding a hunger in these people's hearts for reality.

Between flights into the north we always had other work to take care of. There were the fifty hour and one hundred hour checks to do on the plane, work on the docks to keep them in repair, letters to answer in the office, financial books to balance each month, supplies to look for, purchase, and pick up. Then each spring and each fall during break up and freeze up periods we had to change over from wheel skiis to floats and then in the fall from floats to wheel skiis.

It was during these times that I would travel south in missionary services and show films of the Northland Mission work. When I was younger I could stand the pace but as I grew older I found it so very tiresome. Each morning I drove my car to the next meeting place. It was anywhere from fifty to one hundred miles. I would unload all my things, usually three or four suitcases and three or four boxes of things, carry everything into the church, set up the total display, polar bear, many other animal hides, Indian handicraft work, Eskimo soapstone carvings, set up projector, screen, get everything ready, have a bit of supper and then into the missionary service which usually lasted at least two hours, after which crowds gathered to look at the display and ask questions.

After everything was over I had to gather up my things, pack them in the suitcases and boxes, carry them out to my car, load them and then drive to the pastor's home or motel for a few hours rest. This went on day after day, week after week, into one and a half or two months. But I did meet some very wonderful people.

On June 1st, 1964, Rev. and Mrs. Harold Howarth arrived to pastor the church at Moosonee and be principal of the Bible School each summer. Brian Steed was now helping with the work and took a big load off my shoulders. He piloted the plane and flew north, brought students to the Bible School and helped type letters and bulletins in the office.

CHAPTER 18

TO THE LAND OF THE ESKIMO
". . . .Call upon me in the day of trouble:
I will deliver thee. . ." Psalm 50: 15

Rev. Earl Bergman arrived at South Porcupine by train to accompany me on a flight north on February 15, 1965. We purchased supplies, prepared the plane and on the 16th we flew north to Moosonee on James Bay where we held a service. On the 17th the weather was fair so we flew on north up the east coast of James Bay, on north to the Hudson Bay to Great Whale River. We participated in a service in the Anglican Church there. The next day we flew north to Port Harrison where we conducted a service in an Eskimo home. The temperature was forty below zero and the winds blew across the open, treeless tundra, creating a wind chill of at least equal to sixty below zero.

On the 19th we continued on north to Povungnituk. It was hard to fly VFR in the almost total "white out" condition. No landing strips available, but we landed on the rivers which flowed into Hudson Bay. We visited a number of homes here and had a chance to witness for Jesus. On the 20th we decided to push on as the weather was as good as could be expected. At last we found the small village of Ivugivik. Shortly after landing here, Austin Airways mail plane a DC3 arrived. I talked to the crew members before leaving home about me flying north on this trip. They tried to discourage me saying how dangerous it was.

One fellow said, "You will likely crash into a hill in a 'white out' and kill yourself. At least you'll get lost and we'll have to go out and look for you."

But now here at Ivugivik after they landed, they greeted me and said, "well, I see you've got this far, but be careful, because it's worse farther on." We helped them unload the

DC-3 and load up with freight going out and they took off. We didn't find out till about a week later, but after leaving Ivugivik they got lost themselves. They flew and flew and flew, well into the darkness of night trying to locate themselves and at last had to decide to land someplace because they were almost out of gas. I am sure it was the Lord who helped them to land on a lake because with everything white it's just hard to tell if the surface is ice or rocks. Many planes have been wrecked because of landing on rocks or into the side of a hill. But the next day as they radioed out, two stations got a radio fix on them and located their whereabouts and were able to send a plane in with gasoline.

Here at Ivugivik there were three white people: Peter Bolt the school teacher, his wife Francis who was the local nurse and Rev. Trindell the Roman Catholic priest. Peter invited us to hold the services in the school. The Eskimos crowded in and soon filled the place. They joined in singing in their own language while we sang the same hymns in English. It was a great joy to minister to these wonderful people.

It was on February 22nd, 1965 that I visited Rev. Trindel. I asked him why he had not attended the services in the school. In fact I believe he was about the only one who had not attended. He mentioned that he had his own work to do and since the weather was so cold he had to look after the fire in his church.

I said, "OK, if you cannot come over to the school how about if we all come over here?"

He replied, "Why not? You are welcome to come."

So we announced to the Eskimos that our service would be held in the Catholic Church. Again the people flocked into service. Most of them sat on the floor. We enjoyed a lively song service and then it was my turn to preach. I asked Rev. Trindel if he would come up and interpret for me. At first he declined but after quite a bit of persuasion he yielded and began to come forward. I wondered if I had made a mistake. Would he interpret exactly what I would say?

In order to clarify this while he was coming forward I said, "Rev. Trindel, you'll have to interpret exactly as I say, as my Eskimo interpreter is sitting over there and he will watch you carefully." It was a laughing matter and quite a number who

125

understood English laughed, but yet I got my point across.

God gave me great liberty as I preached the Word. After the message I said, "Maybe there are one or two who would like to come forward for prayer, to ask the Lord to save you, to forgive you of your sins and make you ready for Heaven." Instead of one or two it appeared like everyone came forward, knelt down in front of the platform and called upon the Lord.

Rev. Trindel exclaimed, "I've never seen anything like this in all my life."

A severe storm had arisen, winds were blowing hard and a snow blizzard raged night and day. In fact the winds swung around the compass and we had to go out and turn the plane into the wind a number of times. On February 23rd I woke up to find an eerie calm. It didn't appear right for some reason but yet visibility was good and I could see the blue sky overhead. Earl Bergman and I decided to try to fly to Sugluk. After preparing the plane we took off and flew east. In about a distance of thirty miles we were right into a terrific storm. I decided to turn back and we landed at Ivugivik. Before we even got the plane tied down the storm struck and was as severe as ever. I believe that eerie calmness must have been the eye of the storm.

On February 26th four dog teams left for Povungnituk, a distance of nearly two hundred miles. The weather cleared up somewhat on February 28th and we were able to fly to Sugluk where Rev. Chris Williams was the minister at the Anglican Church. We were invited to share in their service and again we felt the wonderful Presence of the Holy Spirit.

March 1st we decided to fly through to Wakeham Bay on Ungava Bay. We tried to get a weather report but radio signals were bad. After refuelling we took off for Wakeham Bay. I tried to get Frobisher Bay on the radio to check weather but after repeated attempts I was about to give up. Then I heard a voice asking if I was calling him. I said, "Yes, Frobisher. I've been trying to get you for quite a long time. Can you get the weather report for me at Wakeham Bay?"

"Oh," he said, "I'm not Frobisher Bay. We are flying a DC-3 to a mining site and we are about forty-five miles west of Wakeham Bay." Well, it was nice to talk to someone anyway. We found the little settlement of Wakeham Bay, buried in the snow. Most of the houses were covered over completely and only a tunnel through the snow led to the door.

The people were glad to see us even though this was the first time we had visited here. We were invited to hold services in the Anglican Church which was packed out for each service. During the day I visited several Eskimo homes. I took Eskimo Gospel records with me and played them for the people. I remember going to one home. Quite a number of Eskimos gathered in to hear these records in their own language. They not only listened to the sound but gathered around and watched the record player as if it was a television set. At last one elderly Eskimo man came over to where I was seated and said, "This is the first time that you have come here."

I said, "Yes, this is the first time."

He said, "Why did you not come before?" Apparently he was thinking of all the Eskimos who had already died and didn't have a chance to hear the Gospel such as they heard on the records and in our services.

On March 4th we took off for Payne Bay. I talked to Frobisher Bay on the plane radio and was told that Fort Chimo weather was 0 0 - but they had no report from Payne Bay. We flew to within approximately thirty miles of Payne Bay and got into a severe snow storm. It was very difficult to fly as we couldn't see ahead, but yet I didn't want to turn back if we could possibly help it. After flying for the time I knew it would take to fly that distance I knew we must be very near Payne Bay - but no sign of buildings or anything but rocks, ice and snow. I began to circle and then I noticed a plane down below us. This must be Payne Bay. No landing strip was marked out but I descended to land as close to the plane as possible. The Lord helped us make a good landing. After getting out of the plane we then noticed a few houses hidden away in the snow banks on the side of the hill. Again the people were glad to see us and we held good services here.

Our next stop was at Fort Chimo where again the Lord blessed in the services. Then we went to Great Whale River nonstop, a distance of approximately four hundred and twenty five miles, then on to Moosonee and South Porcupine. We thank God for His protecting care over us, as at times the weather was not good for VFR flying.

Once between Fort Chimo and Great Whale the weather got so bad that I decided it would be better to find a spot to land and wait for awhile. We were in the area where just a very few small scrubby trees were growing. As I tried to look ahead through the snow storm I noticed a few small trees in a little semi-circle. I thought there must be a lake just beyond these little trees so it would be a good place to land. As I prepared to land on what I thought was a lake it turned out to be a snow covered hill and I was able to pull up in time to avoid a crash. We managed to keep going all the way to Great Whale.

Early in June of '65 I was at Hornepayne. Large crowds attended the services and the place was jammed packed and full. We knew we had to do something to accommodate the people. The question was, should we try to enlarge the present auditorium or should we look for a lot to build on. We decided it would be better to find a suitable lot and build new.

We continued to visit the many settlements in the northland and hold services for the people. At Attawapiskat the house meetings were getting crowded and we needed a place of our own. On August 28, 1965 while in meetings at Attawapiskat I found an empty house for sale. The owner lived in Moosonee so on my flight out I landed at Moosonee and met with the owner who asked $50.00 for it. This I paid on the spot and got a receipt for it. This was the beginning of having our own property at Attawapiskat although a number of people had already accepted Jesus as Saviour in the services held in the homes. We knew that we would have to move the house we bought but we decided there was enough lumber in the building to make it worthwhile. On September 23rd I made application for one acre of land at Attawapiskat at the Lands and Forest office at Kapuskasing. On September 27 Brian Steed and Ed Winger left for Attawapiskat to dismantle the building and to start construction on our new building on the one acre we leased from the Lands and Forest Department.

For quite some time we had been concerned about opening a church work in the growing town of Long Lac. We checked around to see about buying a suitable property in late 1965. But it was on April 2nd, 1966 that I took out an option on a house

128

which could serve as a parsonage and also a meeting place. Rev. and Mrs. Archie Peevey moved here to pastor this new work.

On April 4th, 1966 I drove to Nipigon, another town which we felt ought to have a Full Gospel church. We had visited here before and found some of the people interested. Mr. John Biro, a Pentecostal man had moved in from Port Arthur and had taken over the Husky Bulk plant here. He too was anxious that a work get started. On April 26th Rev. and Mrs. Eli Kahara arrived to pastor this new work.

Rev. Hannaford, pastor at Manitouwadge, made several trips to Marathon, Ontario and held services in Matti Saasto's home. Then we decided we ought to look around for a lot to build a church on. We spent most of the day July 21, 1966 looking for a lot. Rev. Eero Kahara came to pastor here.

November 16th, 1966 we began Full Gospel services in Geraldton, Ontario. Two ladies were our first workers, Misses Marie Hennessy and Rosella Batterman. An apartment was rented for the ladies to live and hold services in. On January 15th, 1967 while on a visit to many of our northern churches, I noticed the Bell Telephone building in Geraldton for sale. I immediately began to work on purchasing this property. On June 22, 1967 I made a trip to the District office of Bell Telephone about the Geraldton property but was told I must contact the Head Office in Toronto. On July 6, 1967 I met with Bell Telephone in Toronto and tendered my bid on the Geraldton property.

On August 12, 1967 Rev. Bill Stevens and Rev. Vern Hatch arrived by train. They were interested in pastoring in the north. We flew to Manitouwadge where Rev. Stevens accepted the pastorate and then we flew to Geraldton where Rev. Hatch accepted the pastorate.

September 27, 1967 Bell telephoned from Toronto that they had accepted our bid of $10,000.00 for the Geraldton property. I asked them when they needed the money as I knew we were in the red about $800.00 The Bell man said, "We must have the money immediately. Do you want to back out of the deal?"

As soon as I hung up, the phone rang again. Another long distance call saying that a relative had died and left her some money so she felt impressed to phone and ask if we needed any money. "Well praise the Lord!" I said. "We sure need the money and send it just as quickly as possible."

When the transfer papers were ready we had the total sum to pay cash for the property.

Early in 1967 we were still checking around Hornepayne for a suitable site to build a church. We looked at some lots which we could buy for $3,000.00 each. We continued and found one big lot which we could buy for $1,000.00 This looked like the deal we were looking for. But still I felt we should wait a while longer.

Then on November 22, 1967 we heard of a six lot block of land for sale. We visited the owner and told him that we would like to purchase the whole six lots. He mentioned that he did expect to get $1,000.00 per lot to sell them separately, but after careful consideration, as he paced back and forth across his living room, I told him to take his time and come up with a price for the six lots. At last he said, "OK, you can have the six lots for $1,500.00." Praise the Lord. God supplied our need again. Another miracle!

I immediately wrote out a statement exactly as we had agreed on. He read it over and said, "Yes, that's the deal." I got him to sign it and Jim Rodger who was with me signed as witness. We do thank God for supplying this need.

On November 23rd, 1967 I drove to Geralton and we moved the pastor Rev. Hatch and all the chairs, etc. into the Geraldton Bell Telephone building which was now the Geraldton Pentecostal Church.

December 21st, 1967 we received the deed to the Hornepayne property.

On January 21st, 1968 Rev. Alex Strong arrived at South Porcupine to go with me on a flight up north. The weather was not too good till the 23rd when we flew to Moosonee for our first service. Rev. Harold Howarth was the pastor at Moosonee and he also wanted to fly north with us to visit one of the settlements. The next day the weather was not too good but after preheating the plane in the twenty six degrees F. below zero weather we took off and flew nonstop to Pickle Lake, approximately four hundred and twenty miles. We had good services here in Issaac Lawson's home and another Indian home where a number of people accepted Jesus as Saviour. On the 27th we flew on to Sachigo Lake in thirty-three degree below zero weather, approximately one hundred and eighty-five miles. Our church building was packed out for the service that night which lasted till nearly midnight.

The 28th was a Sunday and three services were scheduled by the pastor Joseph McKay who himself had accepted Jesus as Saviour in one of our very early meetings in 1952.

I preached to a full house in the a.m. service. Alex Strong preached to a good crowd in the afternoon service and Harold Howarth was the preacher for the evening service. It was always a time of rejoicing as one by one men, women, and young people would publicly take their stand for Jesus.

Next day Alex and I flew on to Bearskin Lake where we held a service in Elijah Beardy's home. It too was packed full of people anxious to listen to the Word of God.

The next day the weather was very good even though it was twenty-two below zero. We got an early start and flew to Big Trout Lake. The service here was held in Mike Anderson's home at noon. God blessed and a few more people made decisions for Christ. In the early afternoon we flew on through to Fort Severn on the Hudson Bay where Gordie Thomas was pastor. Our church was packed full of people. I stayed in the home of the school teacher, George Hubbard, who is a born again believer. He asked us to talk to the children in school next morning before we flew out.

The last day of January the weather was fair so we decided to fly to Kasabanica. Moses Anderson was our pastor here and we held the services in his home. Our next stop that day was Wunnummin Lake where the people gathered in the Anglican church for a service. Again God moved by His Spirit upon the hearts of these people. We both stayed in the home of John Childs.

February 1st dawned clear and cold, forty-three degrees below zero. It took me a long time to preheat the plane and get it going but our time was running out and we wanted to reach a few more places. We flew to Kingfisher where the school teacher asked us to hold a service in the school to which the adults were also invited. From here we flew to Pickle Lake as our gas tanks showed that our gas supply was running low. From Pickle Lake we flew west to Cat Lake and the service here was held in the home of Robert Gray which was packed full of people.

On February 2nd our next stop was Deer Lake, farther west and somewhat north. The Mennonite people have a lovely church here and they invited us to hold a service there although it was the middle of the day. A great crowd gathered in from all directions and it was a wonderful service. The presence of the Lord was so real. Late that afternoon we flew north to Sandy Lake. I was getting very tired by now but after getting the plane all tied down and the engine cover on, the people wanted a service. That lasted till nearly midnight.

We had left Harold Howarth at Sachigo which is the next village to Sandy Lake approximately seventy miles north east so on February 3rd we flew over and got him. Then we flew non stop to Pickle Lake, refuelled, got a bite to eat and off again for Moosonee about four hundred and twenty miles east. The last fifty miles was quite bad weather with fog and snow.

February 4th the weather cleared somewhat later in the afternoon and we were able to fly back to South Porcupine. Mission accomplished!

April 10, 1968 was a big day when our youngest son David and Shirley Bonnell were married in the Waterloo Pentecostal Church. Pastor Jack Shrier assisted me in the wedding ceremony.

May 20, 21, 22 we held our annual northern convention at Geraldton. Before the convention I was able to visit some of the assemblies by car: Nipigon, Marathon, Manitouwadge, Hornepayne, and Long Lac. Then Rev. Robert Argue our Home Mission Executive from the Toronto International office and I flew to most of the northern missions by plane. We arrived back at South Porcupine on June 1st.

February 10th, 1969 Rev. R. Argue, Head Office Missions Department and I met with Mr. Smith of the Department of Transport regarding the purchase of property at Nakina for our Native Bible School. This property consisted of a large house and large lot which housed the officers in charge of the airport, plus a smaller house and lot, plus an empty lot. Our offer to purchase was accepted.

May 27th Herb Greulich arrived from Galt. We flew to Moosonee and picked up Pastor Ken Sweigard and flew straight across country to Nakina.

We started right in to overhaul the furnaces and motors after we had pumped two feet of water out of the basements. We completed the job about four p.m. with Donald Leslie and Lauri Arola helping. Then we loaded our tools in the plane, flew to Moosonee, left Ken there, and Herb and I flew to South Porcupine where Herb caught the train for Galt. We certainly don't believe in wasting any time when a job has to be done.

On June 18th Gerald Sweigard and I rented a Tilden truck, picked up a new deep freeze at Eatons, loaded groceries and supplies which we had purchased for the Bible School. Next morning with Pekka Tuohima of South Porcupine we drove to Cochrane and loaded on ten bags of potatoes in the truck which we de-sprouted and bagged a few days before. While we were busy down here the Howarths, Sweigards and Ron Tryon were packing up furniture and Bible School supplies at Moosonee. They loaded them and a Fargo van on the train and shipped everything to Cochrane where we met the train. We unloaded the furniture and supplies from the train to the truck, removed the van from the flat car and left Cochrane at three thirty p.m. and headed for Nakina. I drove the truck and Ron Tryon drove the van. We arrived at ten p.m. With the help of a few men at Nakina we were unloaded by midnight. We left immediately, drove all night and arrived home at South Porcupine at eight a.m. in time for a good sauna bath, breakfast, change of clothes, and off to Sunday School and church.

July 28, 1969 Ian Winter arrived from B.C. to help us. He had his pilot's licence but needed a float endorsement which he obtained at the local flying club. He was a great help to pack boxes of clothing - tons of them, tie them, address them, and ship them north, as well as doing office work while I was down south in missionary meetings.

On September 13th I was at Lorain, Ohio where Ray Smith was pastor of a large church. I told him before the service that we needed a good canoe, a boat and motor for the mission work. That was on a Saturday. By Monday morning they had purchased a new Grumman canoe, and with two boats and a motor loaded on a truck they hauled them to Windsor, Ontario for me. It looked as if I had to pay quite a lot of duty on them coming from the States but I visited the Customs office in London, Ontario and explained the whole story. They gave me a document of exemption for everything. The canoe and motor were shipped to Big Trout Lake and one boat to Nakina Bible School.

November 11th, Murray Bell of Oshawa arrived. We drove to Hornepayne, made a survey of the new church property with his transit and put in the stakes for the new church building. These six big lots were purchased for $1,500.00 and we give all the glory to Jesus for getting this land, whereas some other single lots were going for $4,000.00.

Bill Reid, Arnold and Murray Bell were instrumental in getting a very good church blueprint, in fact quite a number of copies for us and it looked as if the new building would be just right for Hornepayne. According to our figures we would expect to pay approximately $15,000.00 for the material and trust the Lord for volunteer help to build. Now we had to trust the Lord to help us raise the $15,000.00. While I visited the churches down south and made known the need, Ian Winter was up north holding services among the natives.

A few years ago we built a lovely log church at Sachigo Lake in north western Ontario. At that time the Hudson Bay Store was on an Island in the lake just a few hundred yards off shore and a pole walkway was built for the people to walk over to the store. I wanted to build on the mainland but most of the people were in favour of building on the Island which we did.

Now in 1969 there were rumors that they would like to move the building to the mainland and asked me about it. After further discussion I said, "Sure go ahead and move it over." They had it all planned to take the roof off board by board, and rafter by rafter, then take the logs off one by one, have everything marked carefully and haul everything over to the mainland to re-assemble in proper order. Naturally the roofing paper would have to be replaced and I promised to purchase and fly it in when needed.

It appeared that no one at Sachigo wanted to accept the responsibility of moving the church building. Then Henry McKay, one of the sons of Pastor Joseph McKay announced that God had impressed upon him to go ahead and get the job done. Early in March 1970 I received word to bring the roofing paper in. March 17, 1970, I purchased the roofing material here at Timmins and Ian Winter and I loaded the plane which Ian left with for Sachigo Lake. On March 20th Ian was back and we loaded the plane up and Ian left again for Sahigo with the second load to complete the job on the re-assembled church at Sachigo.

On June 2, 1970 we were at Hornepayne in preparation to begin construction. Murray Bell arrived on the 3rd. We rented a bulldozer and began excavating for the basement. I purchased most of the building supplies from Hearst Lumber yard and had them trucked to Hornepayne. We put in the concrete footings and soon started to lay the concrete blocks for the basement. Pastor Bob Booker and Brother John Kinsley from Michigan did most of the block laying. Merle Mintz of Toronto came up to work and supervise the building project. The project went on all summer and the following winter with various men coming to help from time to time.

In my missionary meetings in Southern Ontario and in the United States this was our main project and the offerings given were to pay for the material needed. I also mentioned the need of men to come north and help us work on the building.

On Sunday, May 16, 1971, we conducted Sunday School and had a good crowd out to the morning service. Rev. Eli Kahara was now pastor of the assembly. Then in the afternoon, a car load of men arrived from the Akron, Ohio area, where I had held meetings. Rev. Horn, his son and some of the other men arrived to help us work. We had a wonderful service that night. The Spirit moved upon the people and many came to the altar to pray and seek God.

We all found a place to sleep, either in the church or in the adjoining parsonage. At four a.m. the next morning - another car load arrived from the Akron, Ohio area. Then while we were eating breakfast at seven a.m., a van load of men arrived from the First Assembly of God Church in Akron, where Rev. Meador was pastor. Rev. Meador was one of the men in the group of eighteen who left Akron, Ohio, after their Sunday night service and drove all night and arrived next morning to help us build.

I invited them in for breakfast and I said, "You had better get some sleep and rest after that long drive." Rev. Meador said, "We didn't come to sleep and rest, we came to work." So away we went, laying tile on the auditorium floor and also ceiling tile, as well as installing some of the electrical system. Some of the men had experience in plumbing and we installed the two bathroom plumbing fixtures in the basement. On nice days we worked outside, installing the colour-lock siding. To make a long story short, that group of men did a great amount of work in a very short time.

On May 31st, Carl Haacke of South Porcupine and Ian Winters, who returned from Bible College in Peterborough to help us in the Northland Mission, drove through to Hornepayne to work on the finishing of the building.

On June 11th, 1971, the dedication of this new church was held with Rev. Homer Cantelon as guest speaker.

CHAPTER 19

MAYDAY, MAYDAY, MAYDAY....

"I will say of the Lord, He is my refuge and my fortress: my God; in Him will I trust." Psalm 91: 2

MAYDAY, MAYDAY, MAYDAY--CF-LGT **Cessna** 180 on skis, crashed on landing--location forty-eight degrees twenty-nine minutes north latitude, eighty-one degrees eleven minutes west longitude, Porcupine Lake, Ontario.

After such a wonderful winter of services all across the Northland, both in Ontario and Quebec, in which many precious souls came to Jesus for salvation, many sick bodies were healed by the power of God, and believers filled with the Mighty Baptism of the Holy Spirit, then this happened. It was such a beautiful sunny day, February 22nd, 1971, and we were flying from Sioux Lookout non-stop approximately five hundred miles at 10,000' altitude to South Porcupine. I circled the landing area once, and then came in. The snow covered surface of the lake was a bit rough, but nothing, compared to many very rough landings in the far north. The plane slowed down, and all was well, so I thought. Then I applied left rudder to taxi toward shore. At that instant the right undercarriage leg broke off at the fuselage, which let the right wing crumble on the snow as the plane swung ninety degrees to the right. Both blades of the propeller were also badly bent. it was a shock, and unbelievable, after such a wonderful flight all through the north with many, many landings on very rough surfaces, and now to get back home and have this happen.

Brother George Whittal, and I got out of the plane, surveyed the damage, and started to walk to shore. A Beaver plane circled over-head, then landed before we reached shore. In it was the Department of Transport Officials, up from Toronto to investigate another plane accident. They said, "You fellows are lucky that you are not injured." They can call it luck, but we know it was the hand of the Lord. I asked them what I could have done to prevent it. They said, "Nothing. You are fortunate that it happened here, and not hundreds of miles back in no man's land." And as I considered it, I realized how true it was. If that leg had broken in some of the places away up north, we could have been stuck there for weeks before another plane would come in. Incidently, "Mayday" is the international call of a plane in distress. This call has precedence over all other radio communications because it is a call of distress. And I mean **DISTRESS.** I phoned our insurance agent in Toronto, then Orillia Airways. Sterling Beaudry, of Orillia Airways, brought up another wing, propeller, and leg by truck. They removed the damaged parts on our plane, and installed the good parts, then flew the plane to Orillia where it was repaired. The insurance company mentioned the cost would be approximately $4,000. Our insurance covered this, less the deductible, plus the C. of A. (Certificate of Worthiness), and a new leg, as it's not good to have one new leg, and one old one. That's what I mean when I mention we are in **DISTRESS.** Now what?

Another miracle I wish to share with you in the same connection--I understand the total cost of the plane accident repair bill was around $5,000. (in most cases the cost exceeds the estimates). Our insurance deduction was $650.00 plus the cost of two new legs, the C. of A., and the work done on the radio and controls which were not included in the accident. Total cost to us could be approximately $1,500.00. In fear and trembling I asked Harry Stirk of Orillia Airways what the bad news was.

He said, "John, I hardly know what to do in this case." Then he added, "How about you paying the $650.00 deductible, and we'll look after all the rest." Well praise the Lord! It didn't take me long to agree with him. Who said God's Word is not true? "Give and it shall be given unto you."

CHAPTER 20

ANOTHER BUILDING PROJECT
"The people had a mind to work . . ." Ne. 4: 6

Rev. Leonard Thirsk of Komoko, Ontario has been a real blessing to the work in the North. He has visited many assemblies and conducted revival meetings. All the people love his bango playing and singing as well as his preaching of the Word. Many have accepted Jesus through his ministry, and many sick bodies have been healed. Leonard has been used of God in a mighty way and feels a special calling to minister to these people.

Among the many settlements across the northland which we visited and where we held services was Weagamow which in English means Round Lake. I have flown there many times over the past many years. Our services were usually held in homes or in the school building. Now the people asked that a church be built. We held a special business meeting for this purpose and they wanted a definite promise from me that a church would be built. I was on the spot. What shall I say? If I said "Yes", then I must be prepared to follow up on my promise. The cost of the material we figured roughly would be around $8,000.00 - where in the world would we get that amount of money? But right at that moment the Lord began to speak to me, "Is this your work or is it mine?" As many people often referred to the work in the north as "Brother Spillenaar's work", I immediately realized that this was the Lord's work and if so, He surely could supply every need. So I told the people, "Yes we will build a church here next summer." It was on August 16, 1971 that we walked through the village with the chief and picked out a site on which to build a church. We decided what size the building would be and made a list of all the material needed.

I placed a large order for all the material in Winnipeg to be shipped by truck and then by tractor train that winter to Weagamow.

In my missionary meetings that fall I mentioned this need. The people responded in a wonderful way and the building fund for Weagamow grew rapidly night after night. I also mentioned the need for men to come north to help us build. I had a good missionary meeting with Rev. Don Holtzapple of the large Diamond Hill Baptist Church in Mansfield, Ohio on April 25th, 1972. He promised to come north with a group of men, also Rev. Horn of Litchfield, Ohio, which is near Akron and Rev. Meador of First Assembly of God Church of Akron promised to bring a few men to help us build.

On April 30th, 1972, I had good services all day with Rev. Eliason of the First Assembly of God Church at Elyria, Ohio and he promised to come to Weagamow to help build.

Pastor Eli Mickenack at Big Trout Lake, had cut two hundred and sixty spruce logs to be sawed up for lumber for the new church building. Pastor Isaac Kanate of Weagamow had also written that they have taken out logs for their new church. Rev. Hord of the Komoka, Ontario, church has sent a large missionary offering to be used for materials for the two new churches. Rev. Dan Tomen of London, Ontario, told me to go ahead and purchase a power generator to produce electricity so that we can plug in power saws and light bulbs and he would pay for it.

Early in June, 1972, I visited a number of the northern assemblies and held services with them. Then on June 10, at eight a.m., I flew to Mawley Lake, there is no settlement there but a summer seaplane base. We agreed with the men in the States that each group would come up at a different time, so that we would not have everyone together at one time. By coming in groups at different times we felt that more work would be accomplished.

The first group agreed to drive the fifteen hundred or so miles and meet me at Mawley Lake on June 10. They drove night and day to make it on time. Seventeen men in all were in this first group from the First Assembly of God Church of Elyria, Ohio with Pastor Edwin E. Eliason. Included also was

140

Rev. John Horn of Litchfield, Ohio. Our Canadian government is building a road across northern Ontario, from Pickle Lake, Ontario to Thompson in Manitoba and this is the new road that these men travelled on. After flying all these men with their equipment to Weagamow Lake, we started right in, to clear the lot of brush and trees. The tractor train brought our supplies in the winter and these were stored in the old school building. We now had to move them from the school building over to our church site. As I mentioned before the logs had been taken out and lumber sawed, so now we had to haul the lumber by canoe to the nearest point on the lake shore and then carry the lumber to the building site. We all slept in the old school building, with our sleeping bags side by side on the floor. The men also brought up most of the food that we needed, which we supplemented with fish caught in the lake.

The second group from the First Assembly of God Church of Akron, Ohio, was to arrive a week later. On June 17, I flew a load of men out to Mawley Lake and sure enough eleven men from Akron were waiting, including Pastor E. Meador. A Beachcraft 18 Plane was here so we chartered it to fly a load in and then bring a load of men out from Weagamow Lake. Everything worked out well and these men were able to do a lot of work on the building project. Rev. Leonard Thirsk and his son-in-law Paul Gingrich of Komoka also arrived and flew in with this group. The third group was to arrive a week later. So on June 24th, I flew a load of men out early in the morning and sure enough Rev. Don Holtzapple and seven of his men of the Mansfield Baptist Church were waiting with their gear. In order to fly all the second gang and their equipment out and the third group and their equipment in, I made a total of ten return flights that one day. The building was going up fast. All the shingles were put on the roof, electric wiring installed, ceiling tiles put in and we stained the outside walls all around.

By Friday night June 30th, the construction was completed and the first church service was held with Rev. Don Holtzapple as special speaker. God blessed in that service as the presence of the Holy Spirit was felt and the people worshipped God together.

Next day, July 1st, the weather was not too good, but I

managed to fly everybody out to Mawley Lake where they had left their cars. I returned and spent the night at Weagamow. I was up about five a.m. and here it was snowing and blowing. I cleaned the snow and ice off the plane and took off to fly to Pickle Lake. It was July 2nd, but it looked more like January 2nd, as I dodged around the snow storms. The ground and bush below was covered with snow. But I did praise the Lord for the great job done by all these men in such a short time. I managed to fly all the way home and arrived that evening.

July 3rd, I purchased Bible School supplies and loaded my trailer and car full. Next day my wife left with the car and trailer and drove about four hundred miles to Nakina where we held the Bible School. I left by plane via Moosonee and Attawapaskat to fly the students to Bible School. As long as the weather is good and we do not lose any time to refuel we can do an awful lot of flying, by starting before six a.m. and sometimes flying till ten p.m. as the daylight is so long in the summertime.

On July 22, my wife and I wanted to make a quick flight home to get some needed supplies and return. The weather was good when we left, but clouds appeared at about 1,000' altitude so we climbed up and over. As we flew toward home I noticed the scattered clouds getting thicker and higher. By the time we were about half way it was a solid bank of cloud underneath us and we were now at 10,000' altitude. After flying a compass course for a certain length of time I presumed we were in the vicinity of home. Now I looked around hoping to find a hole in the clouds to come down through. We flew on, looking for a hole and at last I found one over a lake. We spiralled down as the hole was quite small, from 10,000' to about 200' to the base of the clouds, but where were we? Which lake was this? I circled a few times and then realized the lake was Big Abitibi Lake, about seventy miles east of home. So we had to back track through rain and very bad visibility to South Porcupine.

The weather continued poor till July 24th, so with a full plane load we started back to Nakina. Before getting half way we encountered very bad weather and I had to land on a little lake. We spent the rest of the day and all night sitting in the plane because it was so cold and there was a heavy rain storm outside. Next morning we were able to fly to Nakina and back to the Bible School.

It was on February 8, 1973, when Don Oakes of Kitchener and I arrived at Big Trout Lake, Ontario. We had a meeting with the Indian Chief and Pastor Eli Mickenack, and agreed that a church was needed there. We discussed the possibility of having supplies brought in on the tractor train. February 9th, at Sandy Lake, a business meeting was called and plans were discussed about building a church here next summer. This tour of the north with Don Oakes revealed a definite need especially in these two villages. We visited many other places and had many good services in spite of the extremely cold weather of forty to forty-nine below zero F.

Each year I also made flights up the east coast of James Bay and held services at Rupert House, Eastmain, Paint Hill, Fort George and even Great Whale River on the Hudson Bay.

On May 31st, 1973, Leonard Thirsk of Komoka and I flew to Wawa where we had agreed to pick up Bob Elgin of Elyria, Ohio. He had driven up and arrived that morning. We then flew up to Big Trout Lake which was still full of thick ice, except a small bay which was open water for us to land on. We checked over the site on which the new church could be built. Isaac Beardy who was employed by the Indian Affairs Department much of the time in construction and saw mill work, let us know that he would work on and over see the job of foundation construction of the new church. He did not know exactly when we would be coming in for he was busy for Indian Affairs at another settlement, Muskrat Dam, which is between the villages of Weagamow and Sachigo. I left Leonard and Bob at Weagamow and I flew to Muskrat Dam and got Isaac and his tools and returned to Weagamow where we loaded the plane with nails which were left over from the new church building project here and were now needed at Big Trout Lake.

After I returned to Weagamow the Indian chief came to me with a story that one of his men was missing. All other trappers had arrived back to Weagamow with their catch of beaver, mink, and muskrat etc., but this one man didn't. Here it was June 1st, and no one had seen him for over a month. Other pilots had been told to be on the lookout, but no one could find him. The Chief asked me if I could go out, about forty miles and see if I could find him, or at least find his body, as he was presumed dead by this time. I refuelled the plane and took two Indian men with me. They had shown me on the map just about where we might find some sign of him. We flew in that direction, our route took us along the west shore of a fair size lake. We were really praying that the Lord would help us on this search. Instead of following the west shore of this lake, we decided to change over and follow along on the east shore. About half way down we noticed a man on shore, then a tent back in the bush.

The two Indians with me got excited and cried out: "That's him, that's him!" I circled the plane and landed and sure enough, he was our man! He had plenty of fur but very little to eat, in fact not much of anything, for the past month as he expected a plane to come in and pick him up. Was he ever glad to leave everything behind except his catch of furs and to climb into the plane and fly back to Weagamow. The lost had been found. Praise the Lord!

From Weagamow, Leonard, Bob and I flew on to Sandy Lake to check on the building proposition here. We made definite plans to build here this year.

June 9th, I flew into Sandy Lake with Leonard Thirsk and Paul Gingrich, who had come to work on the new church. Bob Elgin and two other men of Elyria had just flown in, in another plane. On my previous visit to Red Lake I ordered lumber and building material to be flown in by DC-3 and Canso planes. Some of the material had already arrived. I flew across country to Weagamow and loaded the power generator and bench saw etc., etc., into the plane and flew them over to Sandy Lake.

We had a very busy summer as usual with the annual Bible School on, plus the building projects. Big Trout Lake and Sandy Lake buildings were progressing very well.

CHAPTER 21

A LARGER PLANE AND ANOTHER MIRACLE
". . . .prove me now herewith, saith the Lord. . . ." Mal. 8: 10

We had been praying about getting a larger and more powerful plane. After consulting with different commercial companys working in the north, they advised me to get a 185 Cessna, especially because of the long flights necessary in my work.

On August 14th, 1973 Stearling Beaudry of Orillia Airways flew a 185 Cessna up and we made a deal. Here is the story. I asked Orillia Airways to allow me to use their 185 Cessna for a week to try it out. Harry Stirk, the owner of Orillia Airways said: "No we can't do that, but we'll have the plane up there at twelve o'clock noon for you to try it out and decide whether you want to make the deal. Harry Stirk has always used me extra good and now the deal was - he would allow $17,500.00 for my fourteen year old plane and I would pay $18,000.00 difference. Well, I was down at the seaplane base at twelve o'clock but no plane. One, two, three o'clock and still no plane. At about four p.m. the 185 Cessna landed.

I said, "I am sorry but I haven't got time to even look at your plane, let alone to try it out. You were supposed to be here at twelve o'clock and here it is four o'clock and I have to take my 180 Cessna plane and make two flights one hundred and ten miles from here and bring two loads out before dark."

The men said they were sorry, but they had been delayed. But, they said, why don't you take this 185 Cessna plane and fly in and bring your two loads out in one load?

This really appealed to me. "Will it do it?" I asked.

"It sure will," was the reply.

So I took off and headed northeast. As I flew I wondered

what all the extra gadgets were for on the dash and I was trying them all out. Then I wanted to use the radio and call Timmins and file my flight plan. But what is the registration of this plane? I didn't know.

In my old plane I would call on the radio and say, "This is L G T calling Timmins radio". You see, one must always identify oneself first of all. By the way, to me L G T stood for "Let God Through". I felt foolish, here I was flying a plane alone and did not know its registration. But I really liked this plane. Plenty of power, much more than the 180, and it was bigger and I would be able to carry a bigger load.

"Man," I thought, "it would be wonderful to have this plane, but what's the use of even thinking about it, where would I get $18,000.00?"

Just then I noticed a sign on the dash - C F-Q D H. "Oh, that's the registration of this plane," I thought. "Now I can use the radio." But what would Q D H mean to me? L G T was easy "Let God Through", but Q D H, that's really going to be a hard one. But do you know that just in a split second the Holy Spirit said to me, "It means, Quit Doubting the Highest". "Well praise the Lord!" I said, "Thank you Lord for this plane, it's ours right now, because I will not doubt you!"

I arrived at the lake, loaded in the two loads in one, took right off so easily and flew back. I said, "OK, we'll make the deal." "When do you need the $18,000.00?"

He said, "Oh, there is lots of time."

"Good," I thought, "if I have two or three years to raise that much money, plus all the building and Bible School expenses that will be wonderful."

But the man continued, "As long as we have it by the end of this year."

"Oh, oh, that's only four months away." But "Quit Doubting the Highest", rang in my ears again. I said, "OK, we'll have the money for you." And do you know, before the end of the year had come I had to write and tell people, don't send any more money for the plane, it's all paid for. Praise the Lord! We do have a great big God.

It was a joy to fly Q D H, as I returned the Bible School students to their homes late in August. It had been a good Bible

School term, but we still were not satisfied with what was being accomplished. We knew there must be a betterway. Rev. Argue of the National Office in Toronto mentioned that in Africa, instead of bringing students out to Bible School, teachers went in and held Bible Schools in the different villages. Yes, I thought that would be the answer we were looking for. We decided to sell the Bible School property at Nakina, and late in August a buyer came along and we were able to make a good deal.

On October 1st, I flew to Geraldton where Peter and Vivian Laukkanen were pastoring. They found the parsonage very small for their family of three girls. So, with Arne Lindholm from South Porcupine and Ron Oxford of Galt, Ontario, we built a very good bedroom in the basement for two of the girls. This was a great help for the Laukkanens.

CHAPTER 22

ATTAWAPISKAT — THE JAMES BAY PROJECT
"Other sheep I have which are not of this fold:
them also I must bring . . ." Jn. 10: 16

I was on a northern itinerary up the east coast of James Bay, in March 1974, when I received the word that our mission building at Attawapiskat had burnt down. I had been in Attawapiskat earlier and found that an Indian family moved in our mission building, as they had no other place to live. They were a nice couple with three children. I could see that they were keeping the mission building nice and clean. Our assembly was now holding services in the new home of Pastor Michael Sheeshish. It appeared that while the father was out working the mother had gone to the Hudson Bay Company store to buy groceries, and somehow the place caught fire and burnt the three children to death. An inquest was held but no blame was placed on anyone.

We had a little insurance on the building, about $2,000.00 which we collected. Our people at Attawapiskat and I decided that we ought to go ahead and trust the Lord for funds and build a good size church, including a parsonage. We figured it would cost approximately $13,000.00 for material. If we waited for summer to ship material by boat, it would mean that we would be delayed about a whole year in building. No tractor trains were operating, but we heard that a winter road would be ploughed, to haul supplies in to build a new nursing residence as the old residence had also burnt down. We were informed that the same trucking company could haul our supplies at the usual price if we could get them to Moosonee in just a few days time. I arrived home and went to a building supply company and told them my story. They responded immediately and filled a box car with the needed supplies, and got it off right away to

Cochrane and then to Moosonee. Several truck trips were needed, but we were glad to have the supplies at Attawapiskat in short order.

In my next monthly bulletin, I mentioned the need for men to come north to help us build. In the matter of days, a letter arrived from the Elyria, Ohio, First Assembly of God Church, that a number of men were planning on coming up to build. Soon after that a phone call from one of the men of the Diamond Hills Baptist Church in Mansfield, Ohio said that they were planning to come up.

It was March 26, 1974, while conducting services in the different villages in northeastern Ontario, that I landed at Sandy Lake, where we had built the church last summer. The power generator bench and saw table were there, so I loaded them into the plane and continued my missionary itinerary on and unloaded them when I arrived at Attawapiskat.

Ken Sweigard, pastor at Moosonee, was a great help in contacting the trucking company and making arrangements to get the supplies from Moosonee to Attawapiskat. He phoned me near noon one day that the first truck load of building supplies should arrive at Attawapiskat about one thirty p.m. that same day. I hurriedly prepared the plane and myself and took off across country for Attawapiskat. The weather was good here at South Porcupine and also at Moosonee. But when I got within thirty-five miles of Attawapiskat, I flew into quite a snow storm. I hoped that it would not be too thick, but as I flew on it became worse and worse until I couldn't see a thing ahead of the plane at all. I descended to just above the tree tops in order to keep sight of the ground and I was praying that somehow God would help me to get through. It was impossible to navigate and I was afraid that perhaps my flight course would take me just west of Attawapiskat, even a quarter of a mile and I could miss it altogether. So I changed my compass course a little to the east knowing that I would come out to James Bay, if I missed Attawapiskat. It was a very tense time, as I looked downward trying to determine my exact position. At last I crossed a river and wondered which river was this, as there are a number of rivers east of Attawapiskat. On I flew, then I noticed some buildings on an island and recognized the goose hunting camp.

Now I knew exactly where I was. I swung around and followed that river inland and sure enough in a few minutes I was flying over the town. I found the airstrip on the river and made a fairly good landing in about 0 0 conditions. I really was so glad to be down on the ground and I thanked the Lord for helping me.

The first truck had arrived about half an hour before and we had it unloaded and on its way back to Moosonee. I notice in my records that in just one month a total of $5,647.55 was donated for this one project.

The job we did at Geraldton, building the bedroom in the basement, was so beneficial to the Laukkanen family that they asked if a second bedroom could be built. I knew that in order to do a number one job, we would have to replace part of the northwest corner of the two walls which were cracked. On May 28th, 1974, Bill Caldwell of Galt and I flew over to Geraldton (I had just arrived home the day before from southern Ontario). We started right in to work, from early morning to late at night, and in four days had the job completed.

On June 5th, my son Dan, Bill Caldwell and I flew to Attawapiskat to begin work on the new church building there. We had to clear away the burnt remains of the former mission, then stake out the size of the new building. We hauled in some gravel and made concrete pads for each square post to rest on. Our sills were made up and placed on top of these posts. Then our floor joist on top of the sills and the building project got underway.

On July 16th, John Wallace of Toronto arrived and Rev. Eliason of Elyria, Ohio, and some of his men had driven through to Remi Lake, which is the seaplane base for Kapuskasing. I began to fly men and equipment to Attawapiskat. On June 21st, Rev. Ian Winters arrived from Moosonee to fly our plane as I had to take a bus load of people to the Kathryn Kuhlman service in Ottawa. The Rev. Dan Holtzapple and his men from the Diamond Hills Baptist Church of Mansfield, Ohio, were to go by train to Moosonee and Ian flew them to Attawapiskat and brought out the other group of workmen. I was at Attawapiskat on June 27th, working on the building when some of the leading men of town came and told me that two of their people were missing and could I search for them. Apparently other planes had flown over that area of their winter trapping grounds but no sign of the lost men was found. I thought to myself, if I were lost, I sure would appreciate it if someone looked for me. So I told them I would try.

I took our pastor, Michael Sheeshish with me and we flew North along the coast of James Bay toward Hudson Bay, approximately seventy-five miles. We found the river where the trappers were supposed to be. We flew up and down the river a number of times and also up creeks leading to the river, but no sign of the trappers at all. I told Michael that we would have to give up the search, as my gas supply was running low. We were inland at that time, so we decided to follow down the river to James Bay, then along the coast to Attawapiskat.

We arrived at the mouth of the river and I swung the plane southward along the coast. Just at that instant, I thought I saw someone on an island or sand bar in James Bay, just off the mouth of the river. I swung the plane back and descended for a closer look.

"That's them, that's them," Michael cried. It was a moment of excitement as we realized that we had indeed found the lost men. But what should we do now? It would be nice to land and talk to them at least. But the wind was blowing at a cross angle to the river, which was narrow to begin with, plus a heavy bank of fog lay just beyond the little island. I decided to try to land even though I knew I really shouldn't. It was a good landing, despite the strong crosswind and the trappers were indeed glad to talk to us. The fog was now beginning to roll inland and I told Michael we had better take off. I revved up the engine full blast and tried to steer it in the center of the narrow river. I had applied full right rudder to compensate for the wind, yet the plane veered to the left. I shut the power off, but the plane continued up the rocky river bank and came to rest abut four feet up the bank, sitting at forty-five degree tilt on the bank.

Man oh man, you can imagine my feelings. This was the first time in my life that I ever had anything like this happen to me. We examined the floats and found big gashes in both of them. We straightened out the metal as much as we could and I got some of our winter clothing and stuffed the cracks. Then I told Michael that perhaps if I was alone, maybe I could take off. Michael was willing to stay with the trappers if I would report at Attawapiskat and ask some men to come up with canoes to get them.

We turned the plane around to head for the water and put some poles under the floats. I started the engine with a prayer to God for help and opened the throttle full blast. Praise the Lord! I was in the air and headed for Attawapiskat! I knew I couldn't land out in the river as the pontoons would soon fill with water and sink. I knew the only way would be to land toward shore and to keep the plane going fast and run right up on shore, no rocks here just sand and clay. Again I prayed for the Lord to help me and I did feel better as I swung the plane in toward shore and touched down. As I pulled up on shore the Baptist men who had been working on the church building were right there. I told them what happened. We found the lost trappers but now the pontoons were badly damaged. I arranged for native men to go north and to bring out Michael and the trappers. Then we carried kegs of gasoline down to the plane and refuelled. I wanted enough gas to take me nonstop to South Porcupine. We pumped water out of the pontoons but they filled up again almost as fast as we could pump water out. We turned the plane around and I climbed in and started the engine. The Baptist men shoved, as I opened the trottle full wide again and I was airborne and headed south for home.

I felt somewhat better but really sick in my stomach to realize what a fool I had been to land in that narrow river and cause so much damage. I was climbing normally as I flew south, but then the engine began to spit, sputter and cough until it almost quit. "Oh, oh, now what?" I quickly checked around for a place to land and sure enough there was a fair size river ahead and within gliding distance. But I knew I had to land close to the shore or the plane would sink. Again the Lord helped me and I was able to pull in close to shore. I jumped out with a rope in my hand and tied one end to the float and pulled the plane as close to shore as possible.

"Well, thank God I am safe and no more damage to the plane. But what can I do now?" My flight notification was still active, as I had planned to be back outside by the next night.

The days are long up here this time of the year, so I decided the only way now was for someone to rescue me. I turned my radio on and tuned to 122.8, which most planes operate on in this area and I called and called and called, but no answer. I switched to 126.7 which I use with Timmins and Kapuskasing and most other airports and also the bigger planes would be tuned to this frequency. Again I called, called, called, but no answer. I switched to the emergency frequency, which is reserved only for a time of trouble, 121.5 and called, called and called till darkness but no answer. Next day starting at daylight I tried again on the three frequencies but no answer all day long.

What a feeling comes over one when after calling, calling and calling I listened for an answer, but listened in vain. No answer came in that long second day. The weather was warm and I had plenty of river water to drink and I also had survival concentrated foods in the plane, but I wasn't hungry. I took a pilot biscuit in the morning and then another at night. The mosquitos and black flies were terrible. After shutting the doors and windows at night, I killed all the mosquitos and flies that I could then I sprayed some "Off" around the cabin and tried to get some sleep. But it was not long before a number of these insects were flying around again. On the third day I began calling again. I realized the plane battery must be getting low on power by now, but somehow I hoped that someone, somewhere would pick up my signal. I knew I was off the "beaten path" as I hadn't seen nor heard any planes - all the time I was down. In the afternoon of that third day as I repeated my radio calls, suddenly I heard a voice, yes, someone was answering me, could this be for real? Tears of joy filled my eyes as I excitedly called again. Now the answer came through loud and clear. It was a pilot on a DC-3.

I told him my predicament and asked him to first of all close my flight notification, then to see if he could send a float plane in for me. He said he would, then the signals faded out. Later on that afternoon I called again. Another DC-3 pilot answered. He confirmed my report and said that an Otter plane would be coming in that evening. I told him just about where I was located and asked him to turn off his course and check to find my location for sure, to tell to the Otter pilot. He flew over in

153

about ten minutes times and he said, "You are exactly in the place you thought you were."

It was getting toward evening and I was beginning to wonder if I had to spend another night out. I tried to call a few times hoping to pick up the Otter pilot. At last I was rewarded. The pilot said he was on his way and would arrive shortly. Man, I was getting excited. At last I heard the Otter coming, then at five thirty p.m., he flew over.

On the radio he said, "I don't like the looks of it at all." "I don't think I should put this Otter down there."

"Listen," I said, "I have been here three days already, if you can possibly come in at all I'd appreciate it." Man, was I ever glad as I watched him circle and come in for a landing. I locked my airplane, took my brief case and hurried down river to where a log was jutting into the river. He pulled up to the end of the log, which was quite a feat, as the current of water was very swift. I jumped off the log and onto the float as he pulled away. Man, what a relief, what a feeling of comfort and security as I climbed into the Otter! It took both its captain and co-pilot to handle the plane on take off. We flew over to Attawapiskat as it was time for the eight Baptist men to come out and return home.

What a load we had - 11 men altogether - with all their gear. I wondered if we could ever get airborne. The captain opened full throttle as we manoeuvered upriver for take off. It took along time to get up on the step, then another long time to lift clear of the water. We held just off the water for a long distance as we gathered speed - then a little more altitude till we were high enough to clear the trees before we swung around and headed for Moosonee.

From Moosonee the next morning I phoned down to Orillia Airways. Sterling Beaudry flew up in a Cessna with amphibious floats, picked me up, and we flew over to where my plane was. After checking it thoroughly we removed the fuel injectors and cleaned them thoroughly, and then he made an adjustment on one magneto.

He said, "OK, try it now." I turned the switch on - but nothing happened, my battery was almost dead. We removed the battery from his plane, connected it to mine, and the engine started on first try. Now it looked as if the engine was OK once again. But now the next problem was to fix the pontoons, even temporarily. We flew over to Attawapiskat and got a few men to come and help us pull the plane out of the water. We also used a winch. Sterling put some patches on, and on the second day, we had it airborne and flew it to Orillia for proper repairs. Such is the life of a flying 'missionary in northern Canada.

But we do thank the Lord for so many men and women and young people - even children, who had a part in the missionary work of the Northland.

Before I flew QDH to Orillia for repairs, I knew it would take a few weeks before the plane would fly again. In the meantime, what could we do? It was our busy time, not only with the building project, but also to fly the Bible School teachers to the villages in the north.

A very good friend of mine Archie McLean of Kingston, Ontario had a 180 Cessna plane. Archie had helped us a great deal financially over the years so I phoned him and told him my predicament. He said, "John, come down and get my plane and you can use it till yours is ready to fly again." Well praise the Lord - another answer to prayer. So when I flew QDH to Orillia, I went over to Kingston by bus and flew Archie's KZX 180 Cessna north. It was on July 6th, 1974. It took a lot of flying in all kinds of weather - to fly the two teams of two teachers each to a total of seven settlements where a two week Bible School was held. We were also privileged to have Doctors Peter and Jean Blenkinsop of Calgary, Alberta come north to conduct special meetings at this time - as well as Leonard Thirsk of Komoka, Ontario.

More work men were needed at Attawapiskat. Ed and Ken Winger of Fort Erie, Ontario came up on August 1st and were able to do a lot of work on the new building here. On August 5th I received word from Orillia QDH was now ready for flight. I flew Archie's plane KZX to Orillia. Sterling Beaudry flew my QDH and I flew KZX from Orillia to Kingston. I had had Archie's plane for exactly a month - and put a lot of flying time in. I asked Archie how much I owed him for the use of his plane. He would not take a cent. Thank God that total records are kept in Heaven - and one day a full account will be given. Both

Sterling and I flew in QDH to Orillia and I was on my way northward again.

Bill Caldwell had been working at Attawapiskat installing the electrical wiring, and on July 27 I flew him over to Big Trout Lake to do the same job in the new church there. On August 7th, I was back up north again and able to fly Bill to Geraldton where more work was required to finish off the bedroom in the basement. Bible School days were still on - which required more flying.

On August 27th, I flew Arne Lindholm and Alpo Palomaki from South Porcupine to Attawapiskat to build cupboards in the kitchen of the parsonage and install trim on all the interior. Arnie and Alpo are good finish carpenters and cabinet makers and were able to complete the cupboards and trim in three long days of work.

It was on October 15th, 1974 that David Mainse and his staff of the television programs, Crossroads, and Circle Square, arrived to shoot a film depicting the missionary work in the Northland. The weather was not too good for flying - with rain, fog, and very low ceiling and poor visibility - but they took pictures of take offs and forced landings with the plane, as well as me building a fire for survival and making camp.

I had an Indian boy, Eddy Buffalo and an Eskimo girl, Mary Tobin with me in some of the pictures. It was quite an event and I had the opportunty of viewing these telecasts in reruns over the following two years.

During the winter months of 1974 and 1975 we were able to visit most of the settlements in northern Ontario, as well as a few in northern Manitoba and up the east coast of James Bay in Quebec. God blessed in these services as people responded to the invitation to accept Christ as Saviour. What a joy comes over a face, when one realizes that he has been 'born again' - that he has come out of the darkness, into the marvellous light of Jesus.

Back in Timmins, Ontario we were privileged to have Bill Prankard of Ottawa come for meetings. Hundreds of people attended these services - from every walk of life. Dozens of people came forward for salvation - and many wonderful miracles of healing were testified to. Some with severe heart problems - were healed by the power of God - as well as numerous other illnesses. One of these Prankard meetings were scheduled for February 28th, 1975 - and I was hoping to return home from the north in time to attend these services.

I was up at Attawapiskat, Ontario in meetings at that time and had Bill McLeod and John Whiskeychan of Rupert's House, Quebec with me. They were able to speak to the people in their own language, and Bill was my interpreter when I preached. The morning of February 28th, dawned clear and bright and we were up by six thirty a.m. We flew on through to Moosonee where we refueled and then I flew Bill and John over to Rupert's House - and I returned to Moosonee. Rev. Ian Winter, pastor at Moosonee, was anxious to bring two of his parishioners to Timmins to the Bill Prankard meeting. So the four of us flew south in time for that great service. Again God blessed, as approximately seventy-five people came forward to accept Christ as Saviour. Many who were sick were touched by the Hand of God and testified that they were healed. Some of them said it was just like a warm feeling going through their body from head to toes and all pain had gone. It was just wonderful to see what God was going.

We spent the night at our home in South Porcupine and next morning, February 29th, we flew over to the Timmins Airport and refuelled. Ian Winter asked if he could fly the plane back to Moosonee. I knew Ian was a good pilot and had his commercial pilot's licence, so I said that he could fly in the pilot's left hand seat and I would ride in the right hand seat. We had a good flight all the way back as it was a lovely day. We arrived at Moosonee in record time and descended for a landing on wheels at the airport. Then it happened: for some unknown reason the plane veered to the right and the wing tip hit the snow bank and damaged it quite badly. The Ontario Provincial Police were called and after examining the damage sent a report to the Department of Transport in Toronto. We were able to get a tractor and pull the plane back on the runway and over near the terminal building. I caught the Austin Airways DC-3 flight back to Timmins. I phoned the insurance company regarding the accident. Then I phoned Orillia Airways to make preparation to get the plane flying again. On March 4th Sterling Beaudry and a helper brought another wing up on a half ton truck. Next morning we loaded the wing on Austin's DC-3 and flew back to Moosonee. We removed the damaged wing and installed the good wing on QDH in time to fly back to Timmins and then Sterling flew on down to Orillia. Austin's DC-3 brought the damaged wing to Timmins where we loaded it on the half ton truck and Dan, Sterling's helper drove it down to Orillia.

It was on March 21st that QDH had its own repaired like new wing installed and I flew it back to Timmins in time for another Bill Prankard meeting that night.

August 5th, 1975 I had the Bill Prankard team on a tour of the north. We held wonderful services in many different villages and now we had arrived at Sachigo Lake. Both the Anglican Church and the Pentecostal Church were too small for the large crowd so we met in the Community Center. It was packed full of people and some had to stand outside. A few planes arrived from other settlements bringing sick folk to the meeting. I'll not soon forget the elderly Indian woman from Bearskin Lake who was carried in and laid on a mattress at the side of the platform. There didn't appear to be much sign of life as she lay there motionless. It was a wonderful service as the power of God was present to save and to heal. Toward the end of the service Bill Prankard walked over to the woman and prayed for her. He helped her as she struggled to get up, then to our amazement she walked unaided across the front of the building. Then she ran like a 16 year old with hands raised to Heaven praising the Lord. She was healed completely! A number of months later I was at Bearskin Lake for a service and I remembered that woman. I asked if she was present in the service. She stood up and gave a wonderful testimony of how the Lord had touched and healed her.

I had a lot of supplies to fly into Attawapiskat and usually I would load up the plane here at South Porcupine and take off on skis, fly over to Timmins and land on wheels and refuel; fly up to Kapuskasing, land on wheels, refuel, then right across country to Attawapiskat. If the weather was fair it was a nice flight and I could return home that same day, but some time the weather was bad, as it always changes so rapidly toward spring time. This one day I had left Attawapiskat to fly to Moosonee. It was snowing quite hard and it got worse as I flew on. I was able to pick up Moosonee radio about eighty miles out and they said the weather was not too good there either. After I finished speaking to Moosonee another voice came on the radio. It was the captain of a DC-3. He asked me my position, so I said, "I am about seventy miles out of Moosonee and I am following the winter road flying just above the tree tops. He immediately called back and asked, "Which side of the road are you on - as I am following the same road." We do get into tight squeezes sometimes - but I was able to continue on to Moosonee without mishap. We do thank God for His watchful care.

On September 9th, 1975 I arrived at Geraldton to find that Peter Laukkanen was out flying in search and rescue. A man from a survey party had wandered off and was lost in the bush approximately fifty miles north west of Nakina, Ontario. There were four planes, two Ontario Provincial Police helicopters and fifty-five men out looking for this lost man. Peter returned home that night and asked if I would fly the co-ordinator of the search with a load of supplies to the base search and rescue camp next morning.

The weather was fairly good next day as we checked the maps in the search area. As we took off and flew north, the co-ordinator said, "It's too bad we haven't been able to find this man before now. With the cold weather and rain he just could not survive this long. But even if we can find his body it would be a great help to the parents of this young man." All the while he was talking, I was praying, "Lord, you know all about the whereabouts of this lost man. Help us, Lord to find him."

About six miles south of the lake where the search and rescue camp was located, there was another lake. We decided to descend and check the shoreline at a low altitude. This lake was curved in the shape of a horseshoe. We followed around intently looking for some sign of the lost man. We reached the end of the lake and I began to circle away. Just then we spotted a man in a little bay on the rocky shore.

"That's him, that's him!" cried the co-ordinator. Tears of joy welled up in my eyes as I swung the plane around to land. He pulled up to the rocks and sure enough here was our lost man. He climbed aboard as I let the engine idle. Then we pulled away from shore and took off and flew over to the rescue camp.

What a time of rejoicing as the men welcomed the lost man. Tears of joy flowed from the faces of his mother and father as they hugged and kissed him. After we had coffee I flew him out to Geraldton hospital where he had a medical check up. The report was that he was in fine shape considering his ordeal of six days without food lost in the bush.

Again we thanked God for helping us.

CHAPTER 23

MY RETIREMENT AND A NEW CHALLENGE
"Behold I will do a new thing . . ." Isa. 43: 19

In January, 1976 I conducted a number of missionary meetings in southern Ontario. For two weeks, a snow storm raged through the whole area. I shovelled more snow in that period of time than I had ever done before. My back gave way and I became bed fast for four days. In fact it was one and a half months before I totally recovered. On January 14, 1976 I resigned from the Northland Mission work and promised to carry on till a new man was found. My resignation was not on the spur of the moment. Back in 1975 I felt that after twenty-five years of full time, active service, it was about time that a younger man took over.

On April 12th I flew non stop to Peterboro, Ontario and met with Dale Cummins regarding the Northland Mission work. He felt that God was leading him in this direction and that he would pray about it.

About this same time I had my pilot's medical check up and the doctor pronounced me in "A 1" condition. I thank the Lord for giving me a complete recovery. Now that I had resigned from the Indian work of the Northland Mission, I began to pray, "Lord, what would Thou have me to do."

A letter arrived from Karl Kristensen, a school teacher of Ivugivik, Quebec on the north west tip of Quebec province, asking me to come up and hold meetings for the Eskimos and that he would pay for all the expenses, in fact if I wanted to bring another person with me, his expenses would also be paid.

I contacted Len Thirsk of Komoka and he arrived on April 15th at South Porcupine. Next morning we boarded Austin Airways DC-3 and flew north to Great Whale River. April 17 we

161

flew on through to Ivugivik where Karl Kristensen met us and had a lovely mobile home ready for us. This mobile home had been brought in by ship as their are no roads at all in this part of the country. In fact this is the barren lands - the tundra of the Arctic: no trees at all for the last four hundred or more miles. We conducted services in the Anglican church and in the community hall as well as in different homes. A few of the Eskimos accepted Jesus as Saviour. We arrived back home at South Porcupine April 26th, tired out but glad that we were channels of blessing for our Lord.

May 8th we held our first Spillenaar family reunion at Niagara Falls, Ontario. Eighty-two relatives in all attended. It was a joy to see most of our immediate relations.

June 1st I flew from South Porcupine to Peterboro where Mr. and Mrs. Dale Cummins were waiting for me. We flew to Pickle Lake to look for accommodation, as Dale wanted to live here and be able to fly out of here in the Northland Mission work. God answered prayer in a miraculous way and a mobile home was purchased. We returned to Peterboro on June 3rd and I flew on to South Porcupine.

Further contacts with the Eskimos in the Arctic led us to follow the leading of the Holy Spirit. What would we call this new missionary work? While in prayer, the Holy Spirit brought to mind the Scripture in St. John 4th chapter where Jesus said, "Lift up your eyes and look on the fields for they are white unto harvest."

Yes that would be our name: "Harvest Field". On June 15th we applied to the National Revenue Board for our registration number in order to issue official income tax receipts.

On June 21st Rev. Homer Cantelon, assistant Superintendent of the Western Ontario District of the Pentecostal Assemblies of Canada phoned and offered to sell me the missionary plane CF-QDH for $30,000.00 as Rev. Dale Cummins is not a pilot and would be using commercial planes. I offered $20,000. He countered with $25,000. We split the difference and agreed on $22,500.00. Now Praise the Lord we have the 185 Cessna plane, "Wings of the Gospel", CF-QDH, "Quit Doubting the Highest" for the missionary work among the Eskimos.

June 24th began another summer of activities in northern Ontario when the Bible School teachers arrived and I flew them and their supplies to Weagamow Lake as I had promised to do. I returned to Pickle Lake where Rev. and Mrs. Cummins were living and flew them into Weagamow Lake as well. After three weeks of Bible School here I flew two flights into Sandy Lake. After getting the teachers settled, Brother Cummins and I flew to many of the northern settlements to get him acquainted with the people. My last flight for Northland Mission was on August 29th when I flew the two Bible School teachers to South Porcupine.

After twenty-five years of publishing, printing and mailing the Northland Messenger, I mailed the last issue on August 3rd, 1975. Shortly thereafter, I issued our first bulletin of "Harvest Field" concerning the Eskimo work in Northern Quebec. God has blessed this work amongst the Eskimos in a very special way. I was at Povungnituk, Quebec on September 13th and stayed in the home of Mr. and Mrs. Zolingo Tookalu. Services would last till midnight at least, often two and three o'clock in the morning. One morning September 17th, the meeting lasted till four twenty a.m. Many responded to the invitation to accept Jesus as Saviour, some with cries of repentance. Tears flowed down these faces. Then the joy of the Lord filled their hearts and with smiling and shiny faces they testified of their new found joy in Christ. Another meeting here on December 3rd was especially blessed of God and lasted till three a.m. From Povungnituk I flew to Sugluk on the Hudson Straits.

Again the Holy Spirit descended and flowed into the hearts and lives of these precious people. They are so open to receive all that God has for them. And the Lord is right there to meet their every need.

It may be interesting for you to know that the Eskimos still eat their seal meat, Arctic Char, Caribou and Walrus as well as other meat raw. The government has built lovely homes for them and each one pays a nominal rent which includes oil for heating, electricity from a diesel plant, as well as water delivery and garbage collection.

With meetings every night, which always lasted till after

midnight, and many visitors throughout the day, by December 13th I was tired right out and I flew south. Tired out but very happy in the Lord, as a confirmation of the call of God into this new "Harvest Field".

I am so glad that I accepted the call and have obeyed the Lord to take the Gospel message to our friends the Eskimos of northern Quebec and the Northwest Territories. **TO GOD BE THE GLORY, GREAT THINGS HE HAS DONE!**

For further information or speaking engagements write:
Rev. John Spillenaar
703-24 Midland Dr.
Kitchener, ON
N2A 2A8